AF248560

FROM SHELLEY TO THE ABSURD

SALZBURG UNIVERSITY STUDIES

SALZBURG UNIVERSITY STUDIES

IS A PROGRAMME OF

THE INSTITUT FÜR ANGLISTIK UND AMERIKANISTIK

PARIS LODRON UNIVERSITY, SALZBURG

FROM SHELLEY TO THE ABSURD

Collected Essays

of

G.J. Zambardi Mall

THE EDWIN MELLEN PRESS,
LEWISTON, NEW YORK / SALZBURG AUSTRIA
1996

Cataloguing information for this volume
is available from the Library of Congress,
Washington, D.C.

SALZBURG ENGLISH & AMERICAN STUDIES
Volume 26
EDITOR: JAMES HOGG
INSTITUT FÜR ANGLISTIK UND AMERIKANISTIK
UNIVERSITÄT SALZBURG, A-5020 SALZBURG, AUSTRIA
Fax N° 0043 66 2 80 44 613

TO ORDER: ISBN: 0-7734-4226-X

Europe and the Commonwealth: The Edwin Mellen Press, Ltd.
Lampeter, Dyfed, Wales
United Kingdom SA48 7DY

North America: The Edwin Mellen Press
Box 450
Lewiston, New York
USA 14092-0450

Printed in Great Britain by Antony Rowe Ltd, Chippenham, Wiltshire

Contents

Giovanni Zambardi Mall (Julian) born and educated in London (St. Ignatius' College and King's College London, 1943-1955). After teaching in London schools and publishing a poetry magazine has taught in Italy since 1963 where he is now Associate Professor of English Language at the University of Turin.

B. S. Johnson: An Experimental Writer of the 1960s *

Bryan Stanley Johnson, Bryan or Johnno, as he occasionally called himself in his books, was a Londoner like myself. I knew him in the early '60s, through publishing a poem of his – 'Dublin Unicorn' – in a small poetry magazine I edited in those years when I was a teacher in London. We were both quite different characters from different parts of London. He from outer West and Southwest London, Hammersmith, Chiswick and Barnes, and I from inner and outer North London, Highbury, Islington and Highgate. We even spoke slightly different forms of local English.

At that time Johnson was a supply teacher in the London County Council state schools, and busy writing, and achieving his first successes. In fact I was often asked to read his typescripts to give an opinion. I remember reading the script of his first novel *Travelling People* and he, soon after, saying to me that Constable was going to publish it after he had had a number of rejections.

We used to see each other regularly every week for nearly two years. We went to pubs together, read each other's writing, danced at parties, went on prowls round the Docks late at night after pub closing time, genuinely interested in seeing how seamy, exotic or criminal life was after midnight. We competed in turning our experiences into writing. I remember writing a poem called 'The Blue Café' about a night down by the River Thames on the Highway, the old Ratcliffe Highway of Dickensian fame, and Johnson wrote a short story about the same experience.

We drove down to the Docks on several occasions. (I believe Johnson was looking for material to include in articles or news reports, as he did some journalism too), and the evenings could often be violent. Drunken stupefied sailors, standing against old wet dark walls, being patted over – "rolled" is the term – by prostitutes or policemen for money or drugs or knives. "Let's

*Lecture delivered at the 5th International Conference on the Literature of Region and Nation, Budmerice Castle, Slovakia, 23rd-27th July 1994.

see what you got, love..." and a blousy peroxided ageless tart would open a Malaysian donkeyman's wallet and drag him off to a café, exuding smells of rice pilaf and rancid tea under the dim light of a 45 watt bulb.

And there in the Blue Café B.S. Johnson got punched up. I shall never know what happened exactly, at that moment my back was turned to look at a table football game that was being played in a corner. It seemed that Johnson had offended a very unfriendly West Indian by putting his foot up on a bench, or perhaps, dressed in a black overcoat, shirt and tie, podgy and with blonde hair, he looked like a plain-clothes policeman. The punch went unseen by me and I just heard a gasp from Bryan and out we ran. Outside police were present with a van or car, I don't remember, and we could feel the tension. In fact there was a sequel, when later the same West Indian tried to cross a cellar packed with dancing couples to get at Johnson. I recount these true-life happenings to show that experience from real life even at seamy squalid levels had significance for BSJ. After a morning's teaching, an afternoon writing, an evening's telephoning, or even an early cocktail party among friends, he still had the energy for a short pub-crawl and a midnight "dekko" (i.e. look) at what was going on in the slummiest part of London's East End.

Johnson was a fascinating, soft-spoken, interesting kind of person who often helped others, thought about problems that beset society, work – that involved religion, love and sex – a "hydroptique" mind as Donne said about intellectual activity, and yet Johnson was a paradox. The very same person, calm, warm as a sunny afternoon would change humour when something upset him, like a clap of thunder in a blue sky. Unexpectedly, you were no longer his friend, but one of this "crass" society, as he termed the social setup in England. He would rail and then break off suddenly, cut all communication, and go away. Yet, yet, after a day or two, he was his cheerful, friendly self again.

He could not bear imprecision, – sloppiness was the term he used, and this notion was forcefully brought home to me one evening. His abruptness was disconcerting and emblematic.

The scene, an Albermarle or Dover Street pub, elegant, soft-carpeted, early evening, in a deserted bar. We order two pints of the best – bitter that is. I was relaxing. The barmaid pulls the beer, and places the pint glasses in front of us. I believe I took a sip. Johnson stood glowering at his glass, "It's short" he said, referring to the beer which did not fill the glass up to the brim (it was perhaps half-an-inch lower). "You havn't filled up my glass". The bargirl did not top up the glass. Of course it was difficult in those days of beer pulls when the beer was drawn up from the cellar below in one pull of the handle to measure a pint with exactness not to overflow the glass and waste beer, and the barmaid had pulled short. Johnson turned on his heel and without another word left the bar. I followed him quickly, not to lose him, and also maybe to get him back to the bar; the beer was alright. Nothing doing. He said later something like he was not having barmaids doing him out of his beer. I don't remember if we ever paid for the beer. Pubs were a stage for Johnson, and I witnessed many conversations and "scenes" in which Johnson was the angry young man.

Johnson like most people was conditioned by his time, surroundings, background and education. He was born before the second world war (in 1933) and was marked by those tragic years. He suffered some bombing, he was evacuated to a country town not very far from London, was educated in local state schools and went to work in his teens. All these details surface at different points in his writings. Later he decided he must go to University and after studying hard by himself, he passed his Latin exam, then a barrier to entrance to some faculties, and entered KCL, – King's College London where I met him soon after he graduated.

Johnson was a thinker, often an original one, a critic of society, a hater of humbug, a rebel in most situations, a resolute actor and organiser. All his novels and other writings show a positive, active, no-nonsense personality, striving to achieve a moral end, to reveal the vulgarity of modern society, its lack of real values, and he does this by showing society as difficult to live in, unrewarding to the individual except on its own terms, teaching us the pursuit of wealth, money-making as the only worthwhile aim. This sole pursuit of material success depressed Johnson, it lowered or even destroyed most other values reflected in culture, art, literature and muffled the natural *joie de vivre* of most individuals. In his mind, everything had been dulled or corrupted by capitalism. He often used socialist or even marxist terms when he was in the mood. At the time he lived round the corner from the house (in Percy Circus) where Lenin had lodged on a visit to London in the last century. For Johnson day to day life and the institutions were subservient to the creed of "getting and spending"; there was too much pride in our material success, too much emphasis on consumer goods production with the result that our democracy was simply based on the values produced by a good standard of living. The utilitarianism of Bentham and others, the pragmatism of Pierce and others, the values of Keynes and others had eclipsed the humanist traditional values, and the result was that the individual had in the majority of cases become a slave of time and production methods. Johnson dedicated his life and writing in opposition to this state of affairs.

His angry young man mood was with him daily, and took some form of expression regularly in his conversation or writing, and it was something more than personal irritation, though this was the prime mover. It was a *saeva indignatio*, a Swiftian bitterness with the status quo, and it included everything. The vicar of Hammersmith had put up a vast poster that could be seen from the new road flyover at the junction, inviting the public to his church with some such words as "Jesus is expecting YOU" on Saturday night at 7p.m. etc. Johnson's reaction to this was, "Now, our local vicar is telling God what to do".

The humour is odd, anarchical and unexpected. But he was not all irony, sarcasm and criticism. He could regret also feeling for himself and exposing his feelings gratuitously. Emotion caused him real pain. In a poem he hurt his hand opening a door for a girl he was once fond of, and who jilted him:

> He smashed his hand
> in opening a door for her,
> and less pain than

embarrassment shrieked through him.
Concealing both,
grimacing as if theatrically,
he asked himself
who he thought he was to go
around opening
doors for anyone, much less for her.

Johnson had a theory of writing. Writers had the world to write about, real-life should be the centre of their art, but it should come from what was in each writer's "skull", it should not be a detached objective description of life, a listing of things and events of pure invention. This kind of art, which for him was Victorian traditional, a Dickensian way of putting a novel together, was out. It was outmoded, old-fashioned and time-wasting. What was essential was that experience should pass uncompromisingly through the writer's apprehension and reaction to it. This would stamp the writing with authenticity.

B.S. Johnson's experimentation is in continual evolution: his use of gimmicks, that is devices of his own invention, the black pages representing death, the grey fuzzy page, unconsciousness, in *Travelling People*, the vast spacing between words, representing the difficulty aged people can have with the articulation of words, and memory-recall. The climax is reached in *House Mother Normal* when an inmate, George Hedbury, aged 89, suffering from many diseases and ailments including "advanced inanition", can only articulate one thought-word, "moving", represented by one printed word on an otherwise blank page, followed by a full blank page representing sleep.

Johnson was for ever meditating and writing on the art of writing. He did not find it natural or automatic. For him it was hard work which finally brought an end-product, an artefact. In his novel *Albert Angelo*, in order to express the alienation of Albert in society, Albert who teaches for a living, yet is an architect – lives a schizophrenic situation which is brought home to the reader materially in the actual presentation of the text. The page is divided vertically – the text on the lefthand side is real time, the portrayal of the classroom with Albert teaching and answering his pupils, his "kids" as they are called locally in London, and on the righthand side of the page, in italics, we have the counterpoint of his thoughts, his mind, his silent comments on the class in front of him, allowing the reader to follow Albert on the "inside" as it were, showing us his mind at work, giving psychological depth to the narrative action.

The plain prose text contains straight references to Albert's architectural interests. In another part of the section called DEVELOPMENT, he sets a design problem for himself:

> But now: an arts centre for a town of half a million...

and further on, considering the problem of the ceiling:

> Back to my board, refitted, refurbished. What about this bloody ceiling? Hasn't anyone else faced a problem like this? Look at books–yes–Mies, Corbu, Banister bloody Fletcher, Frankl, Nervi, FLW, Pevsner, Knowledge a Young Woman should Have, Malory, Beckett, O'Brien, Sterne–oh, what the hell, My problems are my problems: face alone, any others can offer only marginal comfort, relief. (*AA*, p.109)

We note that books, a sign of the intellectual, include literary compositions, and we have a first indication, a lead-up to the section DISINTEGRATION, where Johnson tells us the real point of the novel is that it is about being a Poet. This unmasking, this deconstruction of his own writing comes with the realisation he cannot continue to use the metaphorical mode.

> – fuck all this lying/look what im really trying to write about is writing/not all this stuff about architecture/trying to say something about writing/about my writing/im my hero/though what a useless appellation my first character/then im trying to say something about me/through him/albert/an architect/when what's the point in covering up/covering up/covering over/pretending/pretending i can say anything through him/ that is anything i would be interested in saying – (*AA*, p.167)

There is no punctuation, the flow of the lines is a device to bring the reader into close contact with the writer's intimate thoughts on what he wishes to communicate – and there is a communication problem. This begs the question, is the writer struggling with objective reality, is he in fact a failed writer, because he sees reality too profoundly and then has a language problem? It may be, and this deliberate on Johnson's part, for, after all, Beckett, one of his masters, was only interested in unsuccessful heroes:

> I am not interested in heroism and success. I am only interested in failure,

Beckett told his friend Thomas McGreevey after the last war in 1946. *Murphy*, his novel had been rejected by forty-two publishers before publication in 1938, and *Watt*, a postwar novel, was rejected repeatedly. [1]

Johnson was in the minor tradition of the English novel, represented first and foremost by Laurence Sterne, especially in his novel *Tristram Shandy*, in which authenticity, psychology and randomness of events are among the innovations which mark him as an experimentalist, eschewing the picaresque adventure story. Sterne wrote:

> Shall we for ever make new books, as apothecaries make new mixtures, by pouring only out of one vessel into another? Are we for ever to be twisting, and untwisting the same rope? For ever in the same track – for ever at the same pace? (*Memoirs*, p.13).

The source of material for Johnson is life. His experimentation is simply a renewal of form as for Sterne.

Again I quote from Johnson's *Aren't You Rather Young to be Writing Your Memoirs* (p.14):

> Life does not tell stories. Life is chaotic, fluid, random; it leaves myriads of ends untied, untidily. Writers can extract a story from life only by strict close selection, and this must mean falsification.

And so we note Johnson's strict interpretation of the word Truth, it is equivalent to Authenticity, and writing from one's own experience guarantees this. However the construction of a book, its "rationale", its organization, impose a pattern and a pattern is fabrication and undoubtedly this is, under some aspects, falsification. Johnson quotes Philip Pacey – "Telling stories is telling lies... is telling lies about people..." etc.

1. *The New Pelican Guide to English Literature* – ed. Boris Ford, *8: The Present* p. 164 Gabriel Josipovici: 'Samuel Beckett: The Need to Fail'.

In *The Unfortunates*, a novel about a friend who dies of cancer, Johnson tries to capture the fading memories he has had of his friendship with Tony, a University teacher, and his family when he returns to Nottingham, Tony's city, as a football reporter a few years after Tony's death. But his memories are random episodes, and not a chronological or even logical sequence of events. Johnson wishes to convey his subjective perceptions of the past forcefully to the reader by numbering all his chapters or episodes as 1 – the narrative starts but does not develop – the end, we know, is the death of Tony, but there is no "story", just a series of contacts, of moments together between friends. The imprecise memories are loose-leaf pages, placed in a box. The reader is free to read them in any order – and is in fact urged to. Time does not matter. The experience has its validity in its here-and-nowness for the writer and the reader. We participate reading. The box in which the loose pages are contained has a cover made from a blown-up purple coloured photo of a cancer cell to signal the terminal nature of the disease and the point of the novel – the loss of a friend, and naturally the transience of a life which exists only in the inexact memory of the living. A violent image involving the reader seriously in the theme of the book.

In another book, *Trawl*, we have a drawn-out image of the sea, fishing, food, sex, sea and fish smell, the author's memory of personal love and sex experiences with different lovers expressed honestly in a kind of meditation-confession, as if he were at the crossroads of life and intends to live in a different way in a search for a true love relationship confirmed by the hope that his current girlfriend will be waiting at the port for him, when he returns, as confirmation of the sincerity of the lovebond, a promise of permanency, after a long voyage on the Barents Sea on a commercial fishing trip.

The ship ploughs the Northern seas, and the author is sick, seasick for days: in his bunk his past life comes up continuously, and he realises he is an individual searching: for truth, for love, for a solution to his existential problems, of choice, authenticity, in order to accept life in a valid form of reality, as personal significance. We could say that *Trawl* is a descendent of James Joyce's *Ulysses*, as far as technique is concerned, and Molly Bloom's long monologue can be seen as the antecedent to the long interior monologue in *Trawl*, which is in a sense a prose-poem; there is not a single line of dialogue, not even as a memory contact in the writer's mind.

In *Christie Malry's own Double-Entry*, Johnson's last novel to be published before his death in 1973, Christie summarises the literary situation:

> The novel should now try simply to be Funny, Brutalist and Short.

This could be seen as a prognostication: how many modern novels have used one or other or all of the three elements. Johnson was not going to use the novel form again. On one page in *Christie Malry*, he quotes the Hungarian writer, Széll Zsusza:

> ...the novel, during its metamorphosis in respect of content and form necessarily regards itself ironically. It denies itself. [2]

and then goes on to talk to his main character Christie directly:

> "Christie," I warned him, "it does not seem to me possible to take this novel much further. I'm sorry".
> "Don't be sorry... Why spend all your spare time for a month reading a thousand-page novel when you can have a comparable aesthetic experience in the theatre or cinema in only one evening? The writing of a long novel is in itself an anachronistic act; it was relevant only to a society and a set of social conditions which no longer exist".

In the same chapter (xxi) Johnson in the same conversation with Christie, his hero, or perhaps, as Johnson says, his anti-hero, defines his writing thus:

> "Your work has been a continuous dialogue with form?"
>
> "If you like," I replied diffidently.

The minor tradition in English Literature is that of subjective psychological writing, going back to *Tristram Shandy* of Sterne and extending right down to modern and contemporary writers, who use the mind and its problems, life as a situation greater than the individual, which impinges on and moulds

2. Széll Zsusza, Vàlsàgés regény-Akadémia (Hungary) 1970, p.101 tr. Novak Gyorgy.

every decision. So we see the hero succumb or suffer. Modern philosophies and psychological theories have often indicated these areas, Kierkegaard and his definition of "angst", Freud and Jung; Existentialism, and many other philosophies and psychological theories have conditioned modern literature and modern man so that literature has taken on dark tones, of hopelessness, irresolution, intellectual nullity, a despair so profound and black that conditioned Johnson's writing to the end. He sees this in himself, from Sterne down to acknowledging Joyce and Beckett as models, and lists many other contemporary writers as influences, John Berger, Christine Brooke-Rose, Brigid Brophy, Anthony Burgess, Alan Burns, Rayner Heppenstall, Alan Sillitoe and others, who he felt had given him something valuable.

There is a final point: and that is Johnson's contest with God. It has its roots in early childhood psychologically. An only lonely child who found communication difficult it seems. Naturally shy with adults, less so with his own age group, he stored up a certain amount of diffidence towards the grown-up world and its institutions, school, family, police, church and so on. Fear was born from the wartime bombing experience, but this was not significant. He himself says that separation from his mother and father probably had a greater effect despite the kindliness of his foster mother in the town where he was a London child evacuee. These childhood experiences seem to have produced a component of fear of the future, the unknown which produced instability in his emotional reactions to situations.

This is the reason why so much of his work deals with feelings about experiences, and his emotional reactions are noted in many references to the past in his writings. The perhaps most effective manifestation of this is to be found in his verse play *You're Human like the Rest of Them*, which was televised and also filmed and won several international prizes. In this play, the hero, a teacher about 30, Haakon, has strained his back. In hospital he asks the physiotherapist why his back was made so vulnerable. An impossible question which the physiotherapist cannot answer:

HAAKON: What I want to know is, how is it that/
Since we can obviously do these things/
But our backs can't do them properly?
PATIENT TWO: Yes?/
PHYSIOTHERAPIST: The fact remains that the spine is just not/
Designed to
HAAKON: Who designed it, then?
PATIENT THREE: Why not?/
PATIENT TWO: Yes, why make it like that?
PHYSIOTHERAPIST: I don't know why,/
PATIENT ONE: Yes, why?
HAAKON: Doctors can't answer 'why' questions/
Any more than vicars can
PATIENT THREE: No
PATIENT ONE: Why?/
PATIENT TWO: But who designed it like this then?
PATIENT THREE: God!
HAAKON: Yes!
It's God's fault!
PATIENT FOUR: Another cock-up!
HAAKON: But whose/
Fault is it if you don't believe in God?/
PATIENT THREE: Yours
PATIENT ONE: Your fault
HAAKON: My fault?
PATIENT THREE: Yes, your fault mate, yours!/

The culprit has been found, and Johnson declares war on God. He has created an imperfect world. We, as human beings are imperfect. Yet we can recognise and imagine perfection. We can create a Paradise in our minds if not in reality. But we are unhappy in this state. We cannot believe or love such an indifferent or downright cruel God. Despair takes the place of love. At his best Johnson's strength is stoicism. Life is there and we go on as long as possible. B.S. Johnson was a counter-current rebel in life and in his writings. He would have recognised the validity of the Anglo-Saxon thane's description of life-experience as similar to that of a sparrow who comes in from the dark, warms itself at the fire in the Hall, and then comforted goes out into the darkness again.

Shelley: The Quest: a Visionary Skeptic? *

INTRODUCTION

The traditional image that we have had of Shelley is of a poet who overreached himself, who had bitten off more than he could chew, whose ideas were confused and imprecise: especially so in this century with its reaction to Romanticism, by literary critics and the climate of reaction to 19th century culture. I allude to T.S. Eliot[1] and others who accused him of propounding "repellent" ideas and overwrought or outmoded writing techniques, and of being ingenuous as an idealist; thus creating strong critical disaffection in the literary and academic worlds. Both Byron and Shelley have suffered a new "exile" in this century. Shelley's idea of theology was antithetical to Eliot's in that the Bible is more diffusive in Shelley's writing. Eliot was a conservative politically, and anglo-catholic; Shelley was a radical in religion and politics. Why is this so? According to Morchard Bishop[2], there is a simple answer: the grand manner in art and poetry has been out of fashion, its practice in post-modern art in industrial conditions, with its fragmentation of Time, its analytical psychological approach to contemporary problems of existence, and the disturbing effect of the anguished human spirit, coupled with the vast extension of scientific knowledge and the far-reaching effects of hightech is such that no poet can hope to use the classical epic manner. Shelley is perhaps the last poet to use this ideal grand style in English poetry. Shelley in his century was a victim of literary fashion: he had been the spoilt child of culture, he who had played with ideas and had written in his own idiolect in a misty, mystifying, incomprehensible way, refusing to commit himself clearly at times on many abstract themes, too honest to

*Lecture prepared for the Department of English and American Studies, University of Salzburg Bicentenary Conference: PERCY BYSSHE SHELLEY, 1792-1992.

1. T.S.Eliot "The Use of Poetry and the Use of Criticism", London, 1933, in H.Read, "The Defence of Shelley" in *The True Voice of Feeling*, Faber 1953.

2. Morchard Bishop, Introduction, *The Poetical Works of Shelley*, Macdonald, London 1949.

speculate philosophically. If Shelley seemed the true romantic idealist in his poetry, his life had an aspect which was strongly rooted in action, and the view that we should take today is that Shelley in his own eyes was first a man of action, – his family, a part of the rich county aristocracy as was always evident in his life style. He liked riding, using pistols, and following his fancy as a lover of young women. He was a complete young man who liked an active life, travelling to many countries; taking long walks in London, Wales and in the Alps, and sailing with his friends in Italy[3], always in contact with nature but also with a lively interest in study, classical and scientific – an expert in languages, he read German, Italian, Spanish, French apart from a deep knowledge of Greek and Latin, and a genuine interest in science, magnetism, mesmerism, astrology, physics ... writing a "green" pamphlet on vegetarian diet. He wrote prolifically, becoming a major poet before the age of thirty. For these reasons he can never mirror the image tradition has given of him through Amelia Curran's portrait or the statue of Shelley in Christchurch Priory as a drowned Pietà in evident contrast with his decided way of acting unconventionally, as when he got married at nineteen, or his intellectual honesty resulting in being sent down from Oxford, later going over to Ireland to rouse Irish feelings to react against their English oppressors. He had the courage to speak out honestly in defence of the needy and the wherewithal to be able to do so, and doing so became a pariah in his own family, class and nation, – a voluntary exile.

As a man his biography is a "love story" not with one lover or love, but for life in its widest sense, all known creation. His interest in science was stimulated by his curiosity to understand the secrets of nature, chemistry, astrology, psychology, religion, for experimentation in applying his knowledge of classical poetics to modern romantic mythmaking and narrative writing.

As a man he was mild, generous, loving and protective although highly concentrated on himself, valuing his own thoughts and actions above others'; even so he was well liked

3. On a visit to the Opera at Turin, Shelley appeared with an entourage of four women, three babies and two maids. A scandal in the early 19th century.

by all who knew him well. Byron thought him most friendly, refined and generous. He imitated and was inspired by models: Dante, Milton, Crashaw, Collins, Pope, Lucretius, Aeschylus, and in turn was an inspiration to many poets, Francis Thompson and others up to the late 19th century – Browning, Beddoes, Swinburne, and in the 20th century, Shaw, Hardy and Yeats.

He has been called the English Pindar, and was inspired early on by *De Rerum Natura*; and by the gothic novel, Anne Radcliffe and 'Monk' Lewis. He loved horror stories and read many of them and very young wrote bad imitations like 'Zastrozzi'... and this interest led to an original analysis of emotion, the dark sides of the human psyche which gives psychological depth to his poetry; his prose and poetry is imbued with a mythopoeic creativity, supported by imagery drawn from his wide-ranging scientific and philosophical studies, reflecting his idealism.

But here I want to note how important it is to read and teach another side of Shelley's art. His plays are neglected because they have been considered relative failures compared to his great and also his shorter lyrics. Shelley of course would not have agreed. He considered writing poetry, plays, and philosophical, political prose, criticism and letters to have one aim: to promote a better society within a relatively short time. Writing and public speaking were the only peaceful means of communicating to the general public before the days of radio and TV. Here I make a plea for a different emphasis. Shelley's ideas are reflected in his dramatic poetry for the stage. A re-reading of a judicious selection with the intention of reawakening general interest in school and university might focus interest in social idealism anew. A new approach and a new appreciation and evaluation is called for. His dialogues are between abstract forces of supreme importance. Not being a great portrayer of character, the poetry is a synthesis of ideas. Omitting ineffectual passages, however, the choruses and semichoruses often reveal great lyrics. At a didactic level, they can be used to demonstrate poetic techniques, by underlining the effective use of tropes and the areas and registers they are drawn from: hyperbole, metaphor, symbolism (in Shelley still to be fully understood), metonymy, alliteration, onomatopœia and other rhetorical devices. It is true the odes are perfect pieces, but Shelley's real purpose was to create an ideal society, and he genuinely thought the theatre with its public platform would be the surest and quickest way to instruct people to believe in improving the spirit of society, to create a new ethic. As we all know Shelley lived in exile and being *persona non grata* in England could hardly develop theatrical experience, apart from the inherent difficulty of insisting on verse and poetry in the drama. This is still a problem which is with us today; very few theatrical writers use verse, – an exception being a writer of contemporary theatre alive a few years ago, called B.S. Johnson[4] who wrote a few short film and TV scripts in verse. Shelley's poetic drama is the poetry of cosmology, the Bible, the poetry of faith in political ideals of a young man; an ideal verse aimed at changing the reality of man's social and ethical and deontological attitudes.

THE QUEST

Shelley's quest was lifelong, an uninterrupted questioning the whys and wherefores and becauses of life, especially concerned with the abstract forces. The main question for him though was political, or rather, ethico-socio-political. He had a three-level approach to his investigation of thought, trying to reconcile this solipsism with what was going on around him in society, and with nature which he contemplated and absorbed actively, revealing his interest extended to the whole of creation, including the mysteries of Time and Death. In *Mont Blanc* he realised the terror and fear inspired by the immanent power of snow-capped mountains, and the beauty of its streams, acknowledging the indifference of this force, a Blakean gigantic terrifying power always undergoing change.

4. B.S.Johnson, writer: born London 1933, died London 1973. He wrote and published poems, novels, memoirs, film and TV scripts published by Constable, Methuen etc. He won several literary prizes in various counties including France, Hungary and Australia. He was editor of *Transatlantic Review* for several years.

In *Hymn to Intellectual Beauty* we have the magic of the Alps seen as a stimulus to man's spirit, an immanency first exalted in *Intimations* by Wordsworth. The emotion of terror here is that of awe, magnetic attraction; thrill and fright together:

> The awful shadow of some unseen Power
> Floats though unseen among us.

There is sorrow at loss of contact with nature, and this poem is the realisation that contact with the power of nature cannot but be good for us – an ecology of spiritual health is needed.

> – why man has such a scope
> For love and hate, despondency and hope?

The paradox of life, and doubt that real contact can be made with God and personalised religious values was a constant with Shelley, he suspected that forces abstracted as Demons, Ghosts and figments like Heaven were only empty symbolism. Despite the skepticism springing from no definite proof of the eternity of the spirit, Shelley ends with hope, and serenity.

In *Alastor*, Shelley shows the limits of the isolated spirit, the great poet, the solipsist who lives in his ivory tower, not developing his gifts for the benefit of society to instruct the spirit and mind of mankind, and concludes that this kind of poet or person dies deluded. *Alastor* is an example of a futile unsuccessful quest, started with intention of seeking the ideal behind the reality: it is Shelley's allegory attacking the all supreme Imagination as conceived by Wordsworth. Too much self-absorbed thinking can lead a person to live isolated from society, never able to perceive ideal forms in nature, be they wisdom, beauty or love as eroticism, and to waste away and die alone (cf scene of 'the veiled maiden'). However Shelley is interested in the regeneration of society as well as self, though he reveals self-destructive drives in his mental makeup in the persona of Alastor.

Queen Mab was written when Shelley was 20, in memory of Harriet, his "purer mind" and first wife. It is his first fantasy revolutionary epic harking back to Spenserian allegory with all the décor of the Fairy Queen, Mab of the Spells. However juvenile and imitative the verse form may be, the ideas informing it were not; they were an intense expression of young Shelley's meditations and conclusions on the rationality of revolution of the Voltairean kind – *"Écrasez l'infame!"*. In this poem, he proposes spiritual refinement through purity, peace, altruism: revolution is enlightenment, and the image of a God remains as a part of primitive human imagination, now surpassed. It follows that this God is now the enemy of mankind and must be eliminated as being "demonic". Religious dogma is now a barrier to the freedom of the modern mind. It has created social barriers to be thrown down, and not to be exploited as in the then new industrialization created by the division of labour introduced by the theories of Adam Smith which had created a new slave class in the name of the god of commercial prosperity and the new demon – Money. A new ecology of the spirit was needed, the creation of a refined moral imagination, which would mould a harmonious society on earth based on the intellect and will of man. Love will be law, "unchecked by dull and selfish chastity". All Shelley's unorthodox ideas are set in this poem supported by ample notes revealing Shelley's beliefs in the matter of politics, the Godwinian philosophy of Necessity in an unhistorical view of Time. The poem is a strong vision based on abstract logic; a utopian dream. The new humanity will be led by an unselfish élite class dedicated to the improvement of society.

The attack on institutions is the main radical aim and the enemy is identified as kings, priests and capitalists. Shelley's basic feeling is how can man knowingly commit evil, surely he would have innate higher ideals if he had not been corrupted by stultifying institutions. Necessity would strengthen the will of man to choose progress, to welcome higher spiritual and social values. Human nature was essentially good, only it was excluded from present society: and the true modern hero is really Ahasuerus, the Wandering Jew (who reappears in *Hellas*, the last revolutionary epic), who recognises only a vengeful God, who used his Son on the Cross to express through Christianity his terrible hate of mankind.

The Revolt of Islam, Shelley's second revolutionary epic, is a story about a possible revolution project, to create the ideal world society. But Shelley foresees failure on the ideological plane, because not enough people will be stimulated to join, and its main spiritual impetus will invariably have pacifist leadership and direction. Laon, the leader, will learn through suffering, but he makes the mistake of pardoning the tyrant, who burns Laon and his wife Cythna at the stake. In *The Revolt of Islam* there are scenes of heavenly bliss in another ideal after-death world. The transfer from scenes of bloody slaughter on earth to an abstract paradisal eternity shows the difficulty an audience has to accept Shelley's fantasies as pure literature, when in fact they are speculative. Shelley was empathic and suffered for others' suffering, a hypochondriac undoubtedly. The news that shocked him was the hanging and beheading of three Derby labourers for a "seditious" march c.1818, and it was a goad to his sense of persecution. The public in England was hostile and prejudiced against him for his unorthodox behaviour from the time of his expulsion from Oxford for publishing the pamphlet *The Necessity of Atheism* with Thomas Jefferson Hogg, to his exile in Italy for his ultramodern views on love and family.

The Quest goes on through the spiritual necessity for regeneration – and this was undoubtedly expressed best in the lyric *Ode to the West Wind* one of the finest poems written: the mysterious force of nature destroys in autumn to leave space and time for renewal: we feel this primal irresistible energy and know it to be paralleled in our own spirit; we, like Shelley, sympathise with the need to renew our personalities as time passes, or else we become spiritually dead, bones in a desert to use an Eliotian image. What perhaps was unexpected was the passionate acceptance Shelley reveals for the necessary violence in every kind of change.

In *Prometheus Unbound* Shelley parallels much modern and contemporary dramatic experimentation inspired by classical Greek literature: Sartre. Anouilh, Camus come to mind. He decided to complete, in an updated version, *Prometheus Unbound*, the unfinished drama of Aeschylus' trilogy, with an important variation. Zeus (Jupiter in Shelley's version) is not reconciled with Prometheus, symbolised as a future mankind in

Shelley's play. Shelley's Prometheus revolts against Jupiter, who represents Omnipotence, and is punished for his proud defiance as in Greek mythology. In Shelley's new version, Prometheus is purged of his rebelliousness. Shelley's symbology is rooted in part in Blakean poetry of ideal forms: in Shelley the entities respond to Prometheus' struggle and Asia (the necessary female counterpart in the aspired sexual and imaginative revolution which Shelley propounds through these abstract qualities in the play) does not reach the plane of abstraction except at moments; she remains a creation of nature, who at times represents beauty and love (as when promoted to an abstraction in Act 2).

Demogorgon is another entity who embodies resistance; he represents the repetitive cycle of nature and ideas, the skepticism of 'there is nothing new on this earth', and the limitation of science and knowledge and human reasoning: he represents the darkness of death, perhaps nihilism and rejects lying metaphor: 'the deep truth is imageless'. He leads the attack on God. A kind of Satanic counterpart to God in the Miltonic tradition, but without the negative aspects.

Panthea, Asia's sister has a dream which gives us a partial answer to the quest; she describes what has been noted as the "symbol of the collective mind ...to form an essential unity... intermingled in continuous creative contact" in Duerksen[5]. The description of Panthea's erotic love involvement with the immortal Prometheus, and her consequent loss of direction in the quest is noteworthy in that it shows the evanescent quality of Shelley's vision, and its unacceptability in terms of logic.

> I saw not, heard not, moved not, only felt
> His presence flow and mingle through my blood
> Till it became his life, and his grew mine,
> And I was thus absorbed...
> My being was condensed...
> But now I cannot tell what I seek;
> I know not...

The quest fails at the limits of consciousness; absorption into a divinity seems the final stage, through personal ecstasy, emotion, – a merging with a divine power.

5. Roland A. Duerksen, *Shelley's Poetry of Involvement*, Macmillan Press 1988.

Another aspect of the Quest is contained in the *Ode to Liberty* – a power discovered and nurtured in ancient Athens, where men organised democracy and culture, freely manifesting it creatively in the arts and literature – and where, in Shelley's lyric, it is the seeking of man's harmonious soul, his triumphing imagination. In this ode, there is a striving after mental, ethical kingship over the torments and problems of life to reach a valued stage of existence, where love and justice are seen as the true components of liberty. Freedom will be supported by total love, equity, and the best of the past, and this must create Hope for a better future.

Horrified and indignant over the massacre of protesting workers by the cavalry in St. Peter's Field, Manchester on 16th August 1819, the famous bloodshed at Peterloo, Shelley wrote the *Mask of Anarchy*. Again Shelley attacks anarchy in the form of God, king and law, that is traditional institutions, together with the thirst for glory, blood and gold, which had reduced England to poverty through the instruments of murder, fraud and misrule, which had brought widespread suffering and death to the world. The poem attacks the industrial money-making system which had pauperised the people, and had destroyed their spirit with overwork and inflation, worthless money, paper coin, and corrupt politics. An enslaved people could not rise – only love, science, poetry and thought, spirit, patience and gentleness could restore the nation. And Shelley auspicates a free democratic parliament be born from the terrible blood sacrifice of the massacre. He invokes passive resistance; death shall be overcome by the righteous, and liberty will triumph – 'Ye are many – they are few, –' and the people will 'rise like lions after slumber'.

Epipsychidion is a clear statement of the faith that Shelley has in the power of human love – it is this energy that is sparked off in each individual that can transmute the inertia of the material world, if the individual allows himself to live positively in an almost transcendent relationship with all creation, personalised love will merge into the unity of a great cosmological Love, without denying the permanent character of the original rapport:

Emily,

I love thee...

Ah me!

I am not thine: I am part of THEE.

Love begins on this earth, but becomes transformed by failure and endures in a spiritual form – a glorification. All based on a paradox:

In one another's substance finding food,
Like flames...
One hope within two wills, one will beneath
Two overshadowing minds, one life, one death,
One Heaven, one Hell, one immortality,
And one annihilation...

This is one of Shelley's most positive statements about life as human beings and the form of afterlife that could be hoped for. It shows his personality with its best aspirations.

Referring now to his skepticism: it is more of an attitude or refusal to go beyond reasonable common sense in matters of theology, philosophy and his rebellion against organised life, personal or public, which leads us to detect a radical skepticism at moments in his poems, plays and other writings. Witness these lines in *Prometheus Unbound*:

The good want power but to weep barren tears
The powerful goodness want: worse need for them
The wise want love: these who love want wisdom
And all best things are thus confused to ill.

A despairing vision, implying a basic skepticism. Compare Demogorgon's answers to Asia who questions who made good and bad, and his reply that it is always the supreme power God, who is responsible for hell, hate and sin. To which Asia rebels and refuses to accept this kind of forcing.

Shelley's most successful revolutionary epic is *Hellas*, inspired by the War of Liberation of 1821 when Greeks fought a heroic losing battle with the Ottoman Empire. The final lyric is a paean to Hope for a new society in the future, where, to quote Blake, "*the lion shall lie down with the lamb*":

The world's great age begins anew,
    The Golden years return,

From waves serener far...

If earth Death's scroll must be! ...

The last stanza reveals Shelley's doubt and despair, indicating the basic dichotomy of his view of Good and Evil where evil seems to have the upper hand – surely an unconscious skepticism on Shelley's part, knowing full well (from Hume[6] onwards) that we create our values in the mind:

Oh, cease! must hate and death return?
  Cease! must men kill and die?
Cease! drain not to its dregs the urn
  Of bitter prophecy.
The world is weary of the past,
Oh, might it die or rest at last!

Hellas is a death poem strangely haunting in that it parallels contemporary world despair of ever reaching an ideal society. Especially in the last few years when socialism has been terribly discounted and shown to be far from ideal. And this is just how Shelley felt about the French Revolution when he conceived of a literature to educate man not to lose touch with his revolutionary ideas and ideals.

Shelley recoups ideal figures of good and bad as CHRIST, SATAN, MAHOMET (symbolically the character of Mahmud, the Turkish leader).

The Devil has an important role:

DEVIL Be as all things under the empyrean,
  Mine! ....eyeless old Destiny...

Then follow vignettes of Christ – an emblematic symbol of weakness – as a king who is mocked, sitting on a chair of scorn... Destiny as the viceregent of the Devil's will... with hounds of Superstition, War, Fraud and

Change
Convulsing and consuming...vials of tears...
...The first is anarchy; when Power and Pleasure,

6. David Hume (1711-1776) a Scottish philosopher who stated that human knowledge is subjective and based on sensations impressed on the mind of the individual. Complete knowing of the objective world was thus precluded to individuals.

On Freedom hang like fruit on the green tree,
Then pour it forth, and men shall gather ashes.

Destiny represents a philosophical explanation of the Devil's view of the end of mankind. It is fulfilled by the negative traces of the hounds or messengers of horror of the Devil.

Christ is also seen as a resultant negative, as a source of division and subjection of mankind, since Christianity is a fountain of sorrow, discord and slavery leading to chaos, death and slow oblivion. All this is part of the effects of evil on humanity and nature: men's emotions and nature's seasonal changes. ('hate, terror and poisoned rain' which can be seen as aspects of the ecology of the spirit anticipated). The Devil who represents a rival power to Christ and God derives his force from its effects, represented by multiple, complex imagery. Christ however replies that eternity is a different Time from the gyres that the Devil conceives of:

CHRIST: Obdurate spirit!
Thou seest but the Past in the To-come...
True greatness asks not space, true excellence
Lives in the Spirit of all things that live,
Which lends it to worlds thou callest thine.

Mahomet participates as a critic of Christianity which is representative of the decadence of the Western world.

MAHOMET: Wake, thou Word
Of God....
Be thou a curse on them whose creed
Divides and multiplies the most high God.

The implicit criticism is of the new theories of Adam Smith and the division of labour devoting energies of the nation to making wealth.

Hellas is Shelley's final statement on his revolutionary theory.... But in it Shelley implies some credence in Platonic ideals where the natural world of life and time is only relatively unreal. In Platonism, the world of life, time, that is, whatever in nature is intelligible, is so because of "the formal elements which are immanent in them" – Freedom, Hope, Truth are such signs in Shelley's Platonism (a medley of skepticism and subjective idealism). We may think, following the exegesis of

Hellas expounded by Professor Gerald McNiece[7], that Shelley's ideas have some ontological status in that they have such passionate motivation in revolutionary hopes and ideas using the formal elements of Platonism as a convenient structure transposed to suit his theatrical creation.

With reference to Godwin's influence, Godwin traced a scale from Necessity which brought Grace, and thus established contact with God. Shelley transposed this triad into Love, as a starting point, Beauty the stimulus, to a final state of Delight or Happiness. These represented permanent values for Shelley. Man is partly an instrument of unconscious forces (which emerge as Personal Identity, a Thou, according to Harold Bloom[8]), when mythopoeic instincts are at their peak. At this point we have the true revolution – it is a new idea in the mental moral makeup of an individual.

In *Hellas* Shelley projects a larger cultural awareness (poets must contribute to the destruction of inadequate hypotheses about the nature of God, evil, and immortality) without weakening the "inextinguishable thirst for immortality" which compels men to conjecture about futurity. The greatness of Greece was "a reality not a promise" said Shelley. Then, to confound further the hopes that rebels have of embodying their visions in the world of space and time, Shelley introduces the skeptical and solipsistic idealism of an Ahasuerus (the symbol of the ageless Wandering Jew in *Hellas*) who casts "on all things surest, brightest, best/ Doubt, insecurity, astonishment" and here we have an example of the paradox which was at the basis of Shelley's life, psychology, artistic creation and beliefs; doubt that everything might be a mirage, individual life like a bubble on the ocean of the cosmos.

He himself was an optimist consumed by despair; an image of himself is contained in the psychology of the tyrant Mahmud, a dramatic symbol of incompleteness.

7. Gerald McNiece, *Shelley and the Revolutionary Idea,* Harvard 1969, especially the chapter on *Hellas*.

8. Harold Bloom, cited in McNiece above, p.136.

CONCLUSION

What is Shelley's significance for us today? Apart from the intrinsic value of his poetic writing: its inspired composition rendered in incomparable form with all its magnetic music, its enthralling rhythms, its incomparable imagery and symbolism, its unsurpassable stimulus to thought as well as feeling. The fact remains Shelley is an intellectual contemporary: his interests in morals, society, goodness and evil, his probings of human feelings and thoughts applied to his ideal of the regeneration of society and the creation of a better spirit in man are our strivings too. His quest for the ideal revolution tempered as it was by doubts, disillusionment and, finally disappointment is still our quest, for what was started by the French Revolution, the search for an ideal society of liberty, fraternity and possibly equality, although up to now it has ended in relative failure has nevertheless transformed the world. Despite the excesses of the French Revolution the world has improved trying to learn from its mistakes – this was the fact that Shelley was puzzling over – why it failed, and his extensive reading on the French Revolution gave him many right answers. We too can see in Shelley our poet of the ideal society, of the ideal human spirit, with the capacity of self-improvement through self-reform and self-sacrifice – all his heroes suffer and learn through suffering. They better themselves and enthuse people around them. With Shelley's example before us, we are stimulated to feel the need for imaginative and moral leaders – the spiritual man with poetic and social ideals is still our hero or better our model, for we must all have teachers or models, to avoid isolation, not to be solipsists or anti-social. I think we can parallel our surprise perhaps delusion with the fall of communism to Shelley's puzzlement over the French Revolution's failure. The ideal of the just society has been elusive, illusory and illusive, yet it will always exist for the intellectual and the moral man, but as Godwin and Shelley and many direct witnesses of revolutions have been able to testify, the ideal revolution takes years of preparation and Shelley's final abhorrence of violence, his moderate view of revolution as a gradual process of education of the spirit is still our way of seeing what is a necessary phase in any era of society's progress which cannot be allowed to stand still and stagnate. Change will come willynilly, and true education for it is a training through self reform, the refining of the spirit through moral contemplation of the purpose of our lives. Shelley dedicated his major poetic output to this quest – the development of the spirit and mind of man towards an understanding of the great mysterious forces in nature and human existence. Also, it must be observed perhaps that all material political and social revolutions are doomed to failure in that there is no final revolution but always a revolution in progress. It is not surprising that so-called totalitarian socialisms of various sorts have been doomed to failure when they established a system which did not allow for opposition or progress, or at worst feared change and became more tyrannical than the *ancien régimes* they replaced.

Finally, the quest is for Man's harmonious soul – the triumphing imagination: love and justice are the true elements of freedom. Poetry and thought as precursors to action create the social freedom we need. A politico-ethical philosophy of moral action coupled with a strategy of resistance, which is reflected on the personal level and love and self-reform. History is a process. From perception to action to free selfhood: an ethical awareness will determine correct political choice which will, in turn, liberate and satisfy the spiritual aspirations of the individual.

A better acquaintance with the ideals in Shelley's writing could lead to a new evaluation of his contemporary significance.

A last – didactic – point is that the techniques of his poetry can be taught through the tropes contained in his theatrical works which deserve selected reading and study in combination with the great lyrics. A new didactic approach which emphasizes, through linguistic analysis of structures and tropes, the significance his plays as vehicles of a will to change the world through ideals is desirable.

BIBLIOGRAPHY

Bishop, Morchard, Introduction, *The Poetical Works of Shelley*, Macdonald 1949.

Bloom, Harold / Trilling, Lionel, *Romantic Poetry and Prose*. The Oxford Anthology of English Literature.

Duerksen, Roland A., *Shelley's Poetry of Involvement*, Macmillan Press 1988.

Hutchinson, Thomas, ed. *Shelley Poetical Works*, Oxford University Press 1967.

McNiece, Gerald, *Shelley and the Revolutionary Idea*, Harvard University Press 1969.

Sampson, George, *The Concise Cambridge History of English Literature*, Cambridge University Press. 1972.

Welburn, Andrew J., *Power and Self-Consciousness in the Poetry of Shelley*, St. Martin's Press, New York 1986.

Welland, Dennis ed., *Selections from Shelley's Poetry and Prose*, Hutchinson Educational 1963.

Post Absurd Theatre: B.S. Johnson

Literature, especially of the poetic or rhetorical kind has been identified as a manifestation of deviant writing (cf. Leech, Crystal et al.[1]) and the Theatre of the Absurd (Beckett, Ionesco, Pinter and others) amply supports this rather unhappy definition with its materialistic overtones of anti-social behaviour. With regard to B.S. Johnson's plays, there is, in fact, often violent contrast between stage happenings, his "thesis" and the "ethos" of the audience. In his work, the absurd contrast begins to acquire tones of cruelty and horror.

A description of contemporary theatre by Martin Esslin seems apt here:

> The Brechtian theatre, intent on making the stage into a platform for social research and experimentation had developed a valid new vocabulary for presenting the *external* reality of our world, more efficiently perhaps than the photographic illusionism of the post-naturalistic theatre would have been capable of presenting it; the Absurdists on the other hand developed a vocabulary and a stage convention capable of putting on to the stage an *internal psychological* reality, an inscape of the mind...

That is a description of the contemporary theatre which seems inseparably bound to what is disapprovingly called "experimentalism". Esslin sees this theatre as absurd but essential:

> Far from being a sign of decadence or foolish faddism, the search for innovation, for new methods and techniques, the experiments with new modes of expression in our time, are, in my opinion, an indication of its vitality, its awareness of the boundless opportunities of a world rapidly transforming itself under the impact of new technologies...

1. Leech in *Semantics* and Crystal in *Linguistics*.

G. Leech: "If one of the major roles of language is to reduce experience to order, to 'prepackage' it for us, then the poet is the person who unties the string. It is in this context that the 'irrational' or 'counter-logical' character of poetry becomes explicable." in *Semantics*, p. 43.

D. Crystal: "It is of course possible in principle for a grammar, once it has made the distinction between grammatical and ungrammatical sentences clear, to give explicit information about the structure of ungrammatical sentences (or at least some types of them such as the 'deviant' sentences which occur in poetry)." in *Linguisatics*, p. 222.

A new theatre was seen as necessary because the naturalism mistaken for reality was too superficial and contact was being lost at all levels. Ionesco enlarging the views of Antonin Artaud wrote "it is imperative to 'push human beings again towards seeing themselves as they really are'". The Theatre of the Absurd was concerned with re-opening paths of communication i.e. Beckett was re-proposing metaphysical and philosophical problems; Pinter, problems of the individual and communication in society. In the case of B.S. Johnson we have a step further from the absurd. His plays have a sociological problem at their core which he presents with shock tactics, with anti-conventional methods which label his work as the theatre of violence or cruelty. His satire is often founded on the fear and horror of the situation, and the alienation of the individual from society. He presents the hopeless situation of the individual of sensibility in modern society. B.S. Johnson presents the reverse of Hume's man of sensibility who will order reality, whose personal ordering of life will give subjective satisfaction. His anti-hero will suffer, see the horror and absurdity of reality and the final extinction of his personality in death. Says Laurence Sterne, (a writer whose techniques often inspired B.S. Johnson's novels) about refined perception of the world:

> "Dear Sensibility! source inexhausted of all that's precious in our joys, or costly in our sorrows! thou chainest thy martyr down on his bed of straw – and 'tis thou who lifts him up to HEAVEN – eternal fountain of our feelings!"

The man of sensibility has links with the divine – it is almost as if a serene life depends on good refined feelings. But B.S. Johnson presents the other side of the coin, a negative value for empathy, often while employing Sterne's technique of asides, digressions and jokes which carry bitter irony and mordant satire laced with black humour and iconoclastic attitudes for Johnson's work. Differently from Beckett whose language has a secondary function to philosophy i.e. *Endgame* (1957) or *vide* admirable article in *Analysis* 3/85 on *ill seen ill said* (Beckett, 1982) by C.Locatelli, B.S. Johnson uses language functionally (this does not exclude a poetic function on occasion i.e. in the screen play *You're Human Like the Rest of Them*) where he uses 10-syllable verse lines for protest satire and whose theme is, in the words of Edwin Morgan, the anti-hero Haakon "disturbed, joke-cracking, isolated teacher who is going mad because the world seems at utter variance with human dignity".

You're Human Like the Rest of Them was first written as a stage play in 1967 and presented as a film at the National Film Theatre in the same year. B.S. Johnson uses functional verse as Edwin Morgan points out in his preface to the Penguin Edition:

> Johnson's dislike of *cinéma vérité* can be carried over into the theatrical line-mechanism which deliberately snaps and grinds its gear-teeth through the theme of bodily malfunction and death.

This theme will be taken up again in the dramatic novel *House Mother Normal* with greater effect.

In *You're Human Like the Rest of Them* the language register used is mainly that of medicine, for the purpose is didactic – the patients do not know how their bodies function. The humour is music-hall in its effects – the sheer total ignorance of teacher Haakon and fellow-sufferers before the malfunctions of their bodies. The contrast of ignorance and impatience of the patients and the patience and knowledge of the physiotherapist, and the working-class vocabulary and presumption to criticize God's way of doing things produce humour, black farce even. Here in the following excerpt the reference is to the spine which can be weakened by a slipped disc:

PATIENT TWO: But who designed it like this then?
PATIENT THREE: God!
HAAKON: Yes!
PATIENT THREE: It's God's fault!
PATIENT FOUR: Another cock-up!
HAAKON: But whose/
Fault is it if you don't believe in God?/
PATIENT THREE: Yours
PATIENT ONE: Your fault
HAAKON: My fault?
PATIENT THREE: Yes, your fault mate, yours!/

Haakon, the anti-hero, tilts at conventional people, institutions and ideas; his behaviour is "tiresome histrionics" for other teachers, but he carries on criticising to get his truth about death across, violating the fragile ethos of convention:

HAAKON ...That's what I want to say/
We're all rotting away, slowly rotting/
And for some it's not even slow either/
We just rot, corrode, decay, putrefy/

(the death paradigm has a cumulative dramatic effect)

And there's nothing we can do about it/
TEACHER ONE That's childish rot, Haakon, just damned childish/
HAAKON Because you first realized it as a child/
Doesn't make it childish equals useless/

The title-theme is reinforced in the next scene – in the classroom – again there is violence to the ethics between teacher and pupils. The dramatic movement is played on two levels – class work and what Haakon really wishes to communicate – the ephemerality of life:

We make you/ too many allowances/

Too many for your presumed innocence/
Too many for your snotty-nosedness/
We wrongly emphasize slight differences/
To the cost of common humanity/
For – and let's be very sure about this – /
You are human just like the rest of them/
You are human just like the rest of them/
And your one certainty is that you'll die – /
Our dying is the only certainty/
(*Someone laughs*)

The dramatic immediacy of the gimmicks, or literary devices has the force of dialectic – a continual opposition of authorial ideas against the accepted ethos in the play and of its characters. Some random examples: a simile to bring home alienation:

You are cut off
like a city street-end by the railway

allusion to repressed sex:

(*to a teacher*) Your sort draw the line at actual entry

music-hall style puns

(*to a girl who has lost a purse*) Helen Hunt for it

(*on sex*) I'd like a nice tight Jersey for Christmas (ref. cows)

contradiction:

That's not the point.

It is!

(opposition of cowardice/stupidity).

Puns, repetition, shock imagery, harsh verse rhythms, antithesis of hero/audience, contrastive poles of interest, paradigms of madness, corruption, death (*kill, flaccid, wrinkled, off his squiff, corrode, decay, rot,* (face) *blown off* (by a shotgun), *injured, putrefy*)... The effect is harrowing, claustrophobic, closure to life, typical of the theatre of cruelty. An extended image of horror ends the scene. A locust making itself as difficult as possible to be eaten by the lizard, both in a cage at the zoo, sums up the human condition in the play. The play ends Ionesco-like with a mimed comic apotheosis of Haakon, whose suffering is mock-heroically portrayed. The final deconstruction of the personality or 'anima' of Haakon is grand irony. The deconstruction begins earlier when Haakon says that his truth, his fable is "a parable children, a true one, true". Haakon's discovery that life is a living death is the discovering of a truth – the play can be seen as an extended oxymoron.

In B.S. Johnson's second play *Not Counting the Savages* (Transatlantic Review 1973) a screenplay presents the absurd or cruel anti-hero once more – but with a difference – in the final scene he becomes acceptable. Constructed with shock tactic techniques the climax is a reversal of character from "piggish" to socially useful. The play has a binary oppositional structure at dramatic and psychological levels: egoistic family ethos/social usefulness; badly mannered individual /good surgeon; indifference/empathy. In the mother's speeches we have examples of pathos/bathos typical of a split personality: "Sometimes I feel like a spectator of my own life... outside... you know?". The love/hate relationship between brother and sister is expressed by the sarcasm[2] of Jerry when his sister offers to go and get mother's car – abandoned in a cemetery where the mother witnessed an exposure scene – a sex episode which is the off-stage action out of which the play arises. The mother exaggerates her self-pity – she has been technically assaulted by a "flasher". The husband thinks the incident of no importance and rather comic. The wife's hyperbolic emotion is played on by daughter and son, the one a hard feminist and the other a sycophantic gay. The predominant emotion in the play is hate the father. The iconoclasm of B.S. Johnson is evident at every line: convention is false, eccentricity is valid. The philosophical and metaphysical position of the individual is one of alienation – the grand theme of contemporary literature. The father-husband-surgeon emphasizes this to an unheeding unsympathetic hostile family:

> If it is all chaos, then any attempt to understand it is just useless. Don't's you see? Pointless. Or even if it only seems to be chaos, then trying to rationalize about it is just so much wasted effort! Wasted.

The final scene is deconstructive, absurd, cruel. It is achieved through a pun (the camera close-ups focus on the words *cancer*). The husband/surgeon's name is Noone, and the pun is "no one can save you. Noone can save you, ..." And the finale of agnition – the reversal from a cruel abominable social and family failure, the man is worthy of admiration and respected as a skilful compassionate surgeon.

The third example of B.S. Johnson's writing is classified by him as a novel, a geriatric comedy, but which seems to stand half way between a novel in dramatic form with dialogue, monologue, reminiscent of James Joyce's episodic dramatisation in *Ulysses*, Nighttown, and a radio play for voices. It seems presentable on stage or as a screenplay. *House Mother Normal* was produced in a limited edition of 126 copies by Trigram Press, 1971 and does not seem to be widely known. In his *Memoirs* Johnson wrote:

> What I wanted to do was to take an evening in an old people's home, and see a single set of events through the eyes of not less than eight

1. "She's still trying to win the Duke of Edinburgh's Award for Courage and Initiative."

old people. Due to the various deformities and deficiencies of the inmates, these events would seem to be progressively "abnormal" to the reader. At the end, there would be the viewpoint of the House Mother, an apparently normal person, and the events themselves would then be seen to be so bizarre that everything that had come before would seem "normal" by comparison... The technical difficulty was to make the same thing interesting nine times over since that was the number of times the events would have to be described.

Often Joycean techniques are used – monologue to express internal psychological reality; a statistical slab for essential information; mime and gesture. These methods being halfway between novel and the theatre. The functional plurality i.e. the inner reality of the mind and exterior reality at the level of action and dialogue forms a part of the binary oppositional structure of the work, conceived on a contrastive axis, individual/society; power of the House Mother/powerlessness of the inmates. There is a more Dickensian traditional echo in the relentless satire and criticism of institutionalized social services and the use of literary devices in the satire, the use of the Cockney dialect, typographical devices, a capital Her for the house mother, Gas for a reference to the First World War; Cockney alliterative similes, "deaf as a post, and daft as a doughnut" which make up the popular poetry of the piece; the use of Cockney or hark-back structures: "Well, I never..."; "Many's the time...", chiastic effects, "custard cow, cowardly custard", allusions to the past in the minds of the characters by anaphoric reference to dead husbands...; italics are used for straight real live dialogue and normal print for private thoughts and talk; the humour and irony is often based on music-hall style jokes, i.e.: on the death of an old age pensioner, the House Mother says "I just hand them over to an undertaker who probably uses them for meat pies..." There are moments of feeling: pathos is generated as when Sarah Lamson expresses a wish to see her son before she dies, "I'd like to see him just once more before I pass over, just the once" or the music hall farce when a parcel of faeces is passed round as a "surprise gift". There is also post-absurdian humour – the humour become violent or cruel, "black".

Black humour dominates in the climax or anti-climax of violence to accepted ethics of behaviour. A public show of sex perversion involving the House Mother and her borzoi through the violent paradox of the situation, seen in a dysphoric perspective:

> HOUSE MOTHER ..about the sadness, the need to go farther the better to appreciate the nearer, what you have now... If you are not like our friends, friend, laugh now, prepare, accept, worse times are a-coming, nothing is more sure.

The Home is a better place than the old Workhouse, though the inmates are subordinated to the disgusting House Mother:

> This is my Empire... For I love only Ralphie... I disgust them in order that they may not be disgusted with themselves.

The final paradox of horror and perversion acted by the House Mother is psychologically justified by her – barbarity in our current ethos seems to be moral. The disgust anti-life effect is supported by paradigmatic vocabulary, whose basic seme is decomposition. The sememic field includes: *muck, spit-bowl, yellowy green stuff, dirt,* (lists of) *incurable diseases, revolting, utter filth, scrapings, mice dirt, pain shoots, ooooooo-oooooooh, waves* (of pain),*shit, 'flu, stink, stinking rotten turd, pigswill.*

Even death is a joke – the old age pensioners are encouraged to discuss how they want to be disposed of after death in debates entitled HOW I WANT TO GO or MY CHOICE OF COFFIN and House Mother herself gruesomely lectures on the subject.

B.S. Johnson's work is a dramatic presentation of a modern inferno, and the levels of reality are explicated by different referential levels: people known in the past, past wars, childhood, past and present working conditions. This leads to a frequent use of irony, which is sometimes post-absurdian. Ambiguous. The ridiculousness of the words, perhaps unintended irony (a lot depends on an endorsing or disapproving tone) in the following example depends on the word "good" in "It's good for them, of course" when House Mother with reference to the inmates genuinely feeling they are being mistreated and expressing this by complaining could be defined as "echoic" (the speaker and audience diverge at the words "of course"); and the audience reacts as to a black humour situation, which, however, subtends unhumorous irony. This example comes under D.Wilson's rules for irony, "nos. 8/9 patently false/patently true, where no irony is in fact present".[3] There is also a strand of metaphysics and philosophy "Time does not bring maturity" – an anti-aphorism – and a bitter comment – "You realise which are the important things only when it's too late, that's the trouble" from the mouth of the House Mother, which tend to summarise the theme of the play. Finally the deconstruction of the piece comes when House Mother reveals the un-reality of the literary mode of communication:

> And here you see, friend, I am about to step outside the convention, the framework of twenty-one pages per persona... Thus you see I too am a puppet or concoction of the writer...

3. cf. Turin, 1985 lecture previewing her book – with Sperber – *Relevance, Communication and Cognition,* 1986.

Dylan Thomas' Wales in his Writings *

The basic layer of influence in the rapport Dylan had with Wales lies in his schooldays and youth, in his contact with chapel, especially Sunday School; at school only English literature interested him, and he refused to take school lessons and exams seriously, but reading books and then imitating poems or rather plagiarising – normal enough in aspirant writers – did fix his attention permanently; finally the Bible tradition of Welsh religion, that attachment to reading and puzzling out the meanings of Holy Scriptures. Then, of course his immediate neighbourhood, Cwmdonkin Drive, the parks and streets of Swansea including, and later especially, the industrial area, and in summer the beach and hills beyond – broadly speaking, SWANSEA and WEST WALES was the most important component in his formation.

Critics have long recognised that this had the same importance for him that Dublin had had for Joyce as an artistic and mental and spiritual reference point. Barbara Hardy refers to regional imprinting during his infancy and later to the primal landscape, the natural and regional images which produced the celebration of the past "parables of sunlight" in his later poetry. Raymond Garlick, the critic, refers in this connection to the "distinctive life of Swansea" that is, its importance as a cultural focal point, and later to the fact that "the Welshness of Dylan Thomas cannot be stressed too much". And to quote Dylan:

> I was born in a large Welsh industrial town at the beginning of the Great War: an ugly lovely town (or so it was, and IS, to me), crawling, sprawling, slummed, unplanned, jerry-villa'd, and smug-suburbed by the side of a long and splendid-curving shore where truant boys and sandfield boys and old anonymous men, in the tatters and hangovers of a hundred charity suits, beachcombed, idled, and paddled, watched the dock-bound boats, threw stones into the sea for the barking, outcast dogs, and, on Saturday summer afternoons, listened to the militant music of salvation and hell-fire from a soap-box.

*Lecture delivered at the 4th International Conference on the Literature of Region and Nation at the University College of Swansea, 20-24th July 1992.

Dylan's family came from the country, a family from Carmarthenshire, the Western area of Wales now called Dyfed where, from his father and mother and uncles and aunts he learned much of living and dead relatives. His folk background history had its roots in the family tales and stories linked with railwaymen, preachers, farmers, teachers, countrymen, peasants and other folk and their private lives and scandals, all picturing for us the nineteenth century movement from country to town, and job changes from agriculture to industry.

This created an imaginatively happy childhood which became a recurrent theme in Dylan's poetry and prose writing. In Cwmdonkin Drive the young Dylan wove reality and myth. The poem 'Fern Hill', included at the very last moment in the first collection *18 Poems* in 1934 and worked on as his last poem when he was at New Quay in 1944 is *nostalgia*—a long-felt love for Wales and its nature, as well as a poetic return to thoughts and feelings of a child in a Welsh village long before, to his now dead aunt and uncle; for Dylan, a re-creation of his soul in the spirit of Wales. For Barbara Hardy this poem is the "romantic celebration of the holiness of the heart's affections" and she notes the use of a Welsh intensifier in "lovely and watery" which is Welsh usage of an English word because it has a different meaning in this collocation. Dylan has a "deep sense of region", a "cradle Welsh poet". For Professor Hardy, Thomas was aware of Hopkins' study of Welsh prosody and she states that this links with Welsh 'cynganedd' and the use of connected internal assonance and alliteration. Walford Davies however in a recent study, *Dylan*, thinks that this could not have been a conscious process. A reading of 'Fern Hill' will show us Wales and 'Welshness' in the poem:

FERN HILL

Now as I was young and easy under the apple boughs
About the lilting house and happy as the grass was green,
  The night above the dingle starry,
    Time let me hail and climb
  Golden in the heydays of his eyes,
And honoured among wagons I was prince of the apple towns

And once below a time I lordly had the trees and leaves
Trail with daisies and barley
Down the rivers of the windfall light.

And as I was green and carefree, famous among the barns
About the happy yard and singing as the farm was home,
In the sun that is young once only,
Time let me play and be
Golden in the mercy of his means,
And green and golden I was huntsman and herdsman, the calves
Sang to my horn, the foxes on the hills barked clear and cold,
And the sabbath rang slowly
In the pebbles of the holy streams.

All the sun long it was running, it was lovely, the hay
Fields high as the house, the tunes from the chimneys, it was air
And playing, lovely and watery
And fire green as grass.
And nightly under the simple stars
As I rode to sleep the owls were bearing the farm away,
All the moon long I heard, blessed among stables, the nightjars
Flying with the ricks, and the horses
Flashing into the dark.

And then to awake, and the farm, like a wanderer white
With the dew, come back, the cock on his shoulder: it was all
Shining, it was Adam and maiden,
The sky gathered again
And the sun grew round that very day.
So it must have been after the birth of the simple light
In the first, spinning place, the spellbound horses walking warm
Out of the whinnying green stable
On to the fields of praise.

And honoured among foxes and pheasants by the gay house
Under the new made clouds and happy as the heart was long,
In the sun born over and over,
I ran my heedless ways,
My wishes raced through the house high hay
And nothing I cared, at my sky blue trades, that time allows
In all his tuneful turning so few and such morning songs
Before the children green and golden
Follow him out of grace,

Nothing I cared, in the lamb white days, that time would take me
Up to the swallow thronged loft by the shadow of my hand,
In the moon that is always rising,
Nor that riding to sleep
I should hear him fly with the high fields
And wake to the farm forever fled from the childless land.
Oh as I was young and easy in the mercy of his means,
Time held me green and dying
Though I sang in my chains like the sea.

Later his long friendship with Daniel Jones the composer was the next determinant phase in his youth. They wrote poetry, literary scripts together and Daniel also wrote his music; they organised literary magazines, radio programmes, created their own private cultural activity: a serious pleasure-giving pastime and Dylan comments on the period:

> I thought I could live for ever in that room writing and fighting and spilling ink, having my friends for picnics, there after midnight....

In the short story 'The Fight' in *Portrait of the Artist as a young Dog* Dylan describes this friendship with Jones, giving us a detailed picture of happiness shared by two boys – an ivory tower consortium formed at a mythcreating age. The style of the story, the ingredients of fantasy, the fusion of ideas and wit and humour could only have happened there in a Welsh suburb in young Welsh passionate minds at that particular time – in the 30's. Walford Davies sees a Dylan held by a redeeming memory – a return in Time – remembering how in his youth Dylan and his friend Dan had reacted against suburban boredom, first with culture and later in "self-conscious bohemian release", in the Kardomah café, the pubs of Swansea, and of course in adulthood, in Soho in London and travelling the United States, against number 5 Cwmdonkin with its knitted texts – a life in a "neo-Georgian Glamorgan villa" as Dylan hyperbolised it.

This is his first visit to Daniel's house, after fighting with him and then making friends:

> A woman stood on 'Lyndhurst' steps with a hissing pom, and, stuffing my cap in my pocket, I was off down the road; and there was Dan's house, 'Warmley' with music coming loudly out of it.

He was a composer and a poet too; he had written seven historical novels before he was twelve, and he played the piano and the violin; his mother made wool pictures, his brother was a clerk at the docks and syncopated, his aunt kept a preparatory school on the first floor, and his father wrote music for the organ. All this he had told me as we walked home bleeding, strutting by the gym-frocks waving to the boys in the trams.

My new friend's mother answered the door with a ball of wool in her hand. Dan, in the upstairs drawing-room, heard my arrival and played the piano faster.

'I didn't hear you come in,' he said when I found him. He finished on a grand chord, stretching all his fingers.

The room was splendidly untidy, full of wool and paper and open cupboards stacked with things you could never find; all the expensive furniture had been kicked; a waistcoat hung on the chandelier. I thought I could live for ever in that room, writing and fighting and spilling ink, having my friends for picnics there after midnight with Waller's rum-and-butter and charlottes russes from Eynon's, and Cydrax and Vino.

He showed me his books and his seven novels. All the novels were about battles, sieges, and kings. 'Just early stuff' he said.

He let me take out his violin and make a cat noise. We sat on a sofa in the window and talked as though we had always known each other. Would the 'Swans' beat the 'Spurs'? When could girls have babies? Was Arnott's average last year better than Clay's?

'That's my father outside there on the road' he said, 'the tall one waving his arms.'

Two men were talking on the tram lines. Mr Jenkyn looked as if he were trying to swim down Eversley Road, he breast-stroked the air and beat on the ground with his feet, and then he limped and raised one shoulder higher than the other.

'Perhaps he's describing a fight,' I said."

Dylan was also aware of the ugliness and squalor of industry and the bad conditions of living of all involved in it, especially the ordinary worker or employee. As a young reporter, he mooched around the industrial area trying to get a story enjoying perhaps the need for contact at a different social level: he was interested enough in Swansea as a place to want to know how the other half lived, at first perhaps purely as a personal experience. Later in a broadcast talk on Welsh poets, he told about Idris Davies, a Rhymney poet who wrote about the working class, about as Dylan said the "inequalities of social conditions" and the "unnatural system of society under which they worked....(or rather) they were not allowed to work," and showed a deeper consciousness of Welsh culture.

There is another important layer to Dylan's Welsh makeup, and that is, *the personal mythical Wales – an ideal Wales.* In Dylan there is a *love for Wales, the longing to state it, to communicate this contact* to an outside world, a wider audience, and in his writing he digs out a complex strata from a deeper level of his self, something which is beyond sentiment and emotion though these are involved. In his own words:

> I came to love words more and more. ...my craft and sullen art

which becomes Dylan's only allegiance:

> Some let me make you of the heartless words...(from 'Especially When the October Wind'),

where he talks of the "loud hill of Wales". His view of Wales in the poems is concentric, concentrated, repetitive, hyperverbal, obsessive, deeploving, rhetorical and self-centring often with literary devices at full blast. To mention some: iambics with extra stresses and inversions, assonance, near-rhyme, assonantal rhyme, vowel rhyme, alliteration, associative repetition, synaesthesia e.g. "light" for "life"; he uses catachresis, slang, sprung rhythm, paranomasia, paragram, verbal wit which "is an integral part of emotional pitch, of sensibility, and of vision – not only in Thomas," according to Prof. William Moynihan "but in all poets".

"A writer," said Thomas to Pamela Hansford Johnson either worked "*out* of words," or "in the *direction* of them...poetry should begin with the substance of words" commenting on Clare's poems and complaining that "Clare worked towards them, not out of them, describing and cataloguing objects that met his eyes: In the beginning was the object not the words. (Clare) could not realise, and consequently his expression suffered, that the word is the object." This review in 1935 led Dylan to become aware of the mystery of language.

These are the technical aids for the poet Dylan aiming at creating an elaborate poem; at first struggling for an inner form, and later for a conscious formal structure on a theme which often mixes with other themes or subthemes. In the just mentioned 'Especially When The October Wind....' we have repetitive statements and an intimate texture of sexual imagery, of a biological process; his originality is beyond discussion:

"Where no sun shines... where no cold is... where no seed stirs...where no wax is", and in this way the poet introduces a deeper level: man's existence at the moment of conception, an original theme, but a poem which is also about the embryo, a statement about life being a process, and that death is implicit from the moment of conception. And so there are two interwoven themes...The 2nd theme or subtheme can connect with the religious layer of Thomas's complex personality, evidenced in his characteristic paradoxical expressiveness. In his note to the *Collected Poems* we have an open declaration on his art, his poetic manifesto :

> These poems, with all their crudities, doubts and confusions, are written for the love of Man and in praise of God, and I'd be a damn' fool if they weren't...

His paradoxical mystical fundamentalism is noteworthy, and indicates Welshness in his writing, namely, a mode which can be recognised – W. Davies talks of

> the survival of a radically Welsh mode of thought or sensibility beyond the Anglicization of a second generation,

which is of course difficult to prove:

> Where is no God there man believes
> And where God is his homage turns to dust;
> God who is all tells in His desert gust
> That one man must
> Be all and all be one...

Surely these lines are a good Welsh answer to T.S.Eliot!

In Dylan's short stories, the boyhood world and its exaggerated myths, and the caricaturing shows another side of Dylan's Welsh bardic nature, a side often deplored; it was stagey, gratuitous and irritating as a representation of Welsh life. The characters are seen in this way though, simply because they are seen through the eyes of a lively young lad, the poet's persona, for the story's characters are children, madmen and fantastic poets, blurring the frontier between reality and fantasy, and so we are taken into the characters through the boy's vision of a mythical Welsh village – this magic is often present in his poetry too, and we apprise that the fantastic element is written out of pity and a will to understand – an empathy that for us emerges as the psychology of his writing, and indirectly as the poet's theory of poetry. This can be seen very obviously in a poem he wrote in memory of his aunt, Anne Jones, an old peasant woman – in which the emotional atmosphere is thundery and charged with suppressed power. The force of writing comes across the almost unbearable rhetoric and in the contrasting styles and levels on which the poem is written; the passionate will to understand perhaps has something to do with what in Welsh is called "hwyl" – the emotional power of the preacher.

In *After the Funeral* we have the characteristic blending – the Welsh region and Dylan's Welshness, that is the mood, his poetic attitude, his bitter irony, his *hiraeth*, a "deconstruction" of the situation:

> After the funeral, mule praises, brays,
> Windshake of sailshaped ears, muffle-toed tap
> Tap happily of one peg in the thick
> Grave's foot, blinds down the lids, the teeth in black,
> The spittled eyes, the salt ponds in the sleeves,
> Morning smack of the spade that wakes up sleep,
> Shakes a desolate boy who slits his throat
> In the dark of the coffin and sheds dry leaves,
> That breaks one bone to light with a judgment clout,
> After the feast of tear-stuffed time and thistles
> In a room with a stuffed fox and a stale fern,
> I stand, for this memorial's sake, alone
> In the snivelling hours with dead, humped Ann
> Whose hooded, fountain heart once fell in puddles
> Round the parched worlds of Wales and drowned each sun
> (Though this for her is a monstrous image blindly
> Magnified out of praise; her death was a still drop;
> She would not have me sinking in the holy
> Flood of her heart's fame; she would lie dumb and deep
> And need no druid of her broken body).

But I, Ann's bard on a raised hearth, call all
The seas to service that her wood-tongued virtue
Babble like a bellbuoy over the hymning heads,
Bow down the walls of the ferned and foxy woods
That her love sing and swing through a brown chapel,
Bless her bent spirit with four, crossing birds.
Her flesh was meek as milk, but this skyward statue
With the wild breast and blessed and giant skull
Is carved from her in a room with a wet window
In a fiercely mourning house in a crooked year.
I know her scrubbed and sour humble hands
Lie with religion in their cramp, her threadbare
Whisper in a damp word, her wits drilled hollow,
Her fist of a face died clenched on a round pain;
And sculptured Ann is seventy years of stone.
These cloud-sopped, marble hands, this monumental
Argument of the hewn voice, gesture and psalm,
Storm me forever over her grave until
The stuffed lung of the fox twitch and cry Love
And the strutting fern lay seeds on the black sill.

The Bible, school, chapel, the suburb of Uplands, quiet on the hill, family closeness though not harmony was the early basis of Dylan's Welshness as expressed in his writing personality, though maybe it took some time to surface, some years of being away from these localities to feel what the traditional migrant Welshman had felt through generations of separation from roots. It comes out in his poetry in a subterranean way, it is buried in the catacomb of the past – he knew of this layer of dark caverns in his mind, and he often merges the layers in his imagery – seriously, mystically in his poems, using "familiar parameters" as Dr James Davies concludes in his admirable concise chapter on Dylan's Wales, 'The Picnic in the Orchard', in poetry which for critic George Steiner, who links Dylan's poetry with the late 19th century poets Mallarmé and Rimbaud, is full of rhetoric, cabalistic devices of syntax and imagery, and frothiness. However, to quote Moynihan again

> Thomas himself said everything that can be said about his attitude towards 'cabalistic devices' when he wrote that the most prized expression should be eliminated if meaning demands it, that conscious obscurity should never be allowed to smother poetry...

These are better words than Steiner's, who was right however – Dylan's poetry is certainly not barren. It *communicates*, makes us participate and receive the "loud hill of Wales.....some let me make you of autumnal spells", an invitation to us to embrace the loveliness and power of nature through his words.

Dylan's prose writing, short stories, plays etc were even more immediate, through the use of comedy, caricature, puns, satire which reveal what Wales meant to Dylan's way of writing. Rural Wales had great significance for him – it was his childhood, indelible memories, nostalgia and deep-rooted love, Wales with all the defects that this emotional involvement could have on his writing.

There are two stories that are emblematic of this nostalgia 'The Peaches' in *Portrait of the Artist as a young Dog*, which is localised on his aunt's farm in Blaen Cym; the story of Gwilym, a young man who exercises himself in preaching in imitation of Welsh style preaching "O God, Thou art everywhere", and sex alone with himself.

Dylan the writer sees two boys a long way back in time in the paradoxical context of adolescence of growing up at a particular time when Welsh religion and Welsh Sunday school had significance for him, made emblematic in the boys' play in the decaying farmyard. Dylan said "I was brought up on the Bible!" In fact he attended his uncle's church, the Paraclete Chapel in Newton.

The other story is 'A Visit to Grandpa's', with again the autobiographical context being used as writing material for His Wales, mythical in memory, existing in a way that is recognisable to any Welshman or person who has known Wales. This story is written meticulously, polished, incisive, funny, fantastic and exaggerated, it holds us through a kind of empathy, and we become a part of Dylan's boyhood fears and hopes, taken back in spirit to that time.

The story, a description of Dylan's grandfather's driving his imagined horses in bed, waking young Dylan in the next room in the cottage is our immediate entrance into the world of childhood, and makes genuine successful literature, being a part of collective psychology – we have all been children. We have all probably read how boy Dylan stays with his grandfather and goes on walks with him. On the last day, they visit a pub where grandpa pays the bill with a gold sovereign, an odd touch which reveals a peaceful familiar world that was in the prehistoric past for Dylan the writer. Grandpa disappears and the neighbours set off with the trap and pony taking Dylan to find him. They know where he is, as he had disappeared before and had promised them not to cause alarm again. He is duly found on Carmarthen bridge with his black bag, best waistcoat and old hat in the middle of the afternoon and refuses to return home.

First I'll quote Dylan's arrival.

> In the middle of the night I woke from a dream full of whips and lariats as long as serpents, and runaway coaches on mountain passes, and wide, windy gallops over cactus fields, and I heard the man in the next room crying, "Gee-up!" and "Whoa!" and trotting his tongue on the roof of his mouth.
>
> It was the first time I had stayed in grandpa's house. The floorboards had squeaked like mice as I climbed into bed, and the mice between the walls had creaked like wood as though another visitor was walking on them. It was a mild summer night, but curtains had flapped and branches beaten against the window. I had pulled the sheets over my head, and soon was roaring and riding in a book.
>
> "Whoa there, my beauties!" cried grandpa. His voice sounded very young and loud, and his tongue had powerful hooves, and he made his bedroom into a great meadow. I thought I would see if he was ill, or had set his bedclothes on fire, for my mother had said that he lit his pipe under the blankets, and had warned me to run to his help if I smelt smoke in the night. I went on tiptoe through the darkness to his bedroom door, brushing against the furniture and upsetting a candlestick with a thump. When I saw there was a light in the room I felt frightened, and as I opened the door I heard grandpa shout, "Gee-up!" as loudly as a bull with a megaphone.
>
> He was sitting straight up in bed and rocking from side to side as though the bed were on a rough road; the knotted edges of the counterpane were his reins; his invisible horse stood in a shadow beyond the bedside candle. Over a white flannel nightshirt he was wearing a red waistcoat with walnut-sized brass buttons. The over-filled bowl of his pipe smouldered among his whiskers like a little, burning hayrick on a stick. At the sight of me, his hands dropped from the reins and lay blue and quiet, the bed stopped still on a level road, he

muffled his tongue into silence, and the horses drew softly up.

"Is anything the matter, grandpa?" I asked, though the bed clothes were not on fire.

(Grandpa is duly found on Carmarthen bridge with his black bag in the middle of the afternoon wearing his best waistcoat and old hat)

Grandpa did not answer, but inclined his face to the river wind, so that his beard was set dancing and wagging as though he talked, and watched the coracle men move, like turtles, on the shore.

Mr Griff raised his stunted barber's pole. "Now where do you think you are going," he said, "with your old black bag?"

Grandpa said, "I am going to Llangadock to be buried," and he watched the coracle shells slip into the water lightly, and the gulls complain over the fish-filled water as bitterly as Mr Price complained:

"But you aren't dead yet, Dai Thomas"

For a moment grandpa reflected, then:'"There's no sense in lying dead in Llanstephan," he said. "The ground is comfy in Llangadock; you can twitch your legs without putting them into the sea."

His neighbours moved close to him. They said: "You aren't dead, Mr Thomas."

"How can you be buried then?"

"Nobody's going to bury you in Llanstephan"

"Come on home, Mr Thomas"

"There's strong beer for tea"

"And cake"

But grandpa stood firmly on the bridge, and clutched his bag to his side, and stared at the flowing river and the sky, like a prophet who has no doubt.

Dylan Thomas in Italian

There has been considerable interest abroad, especially in Italy, from the time of Dylan's last writings to today when he is still the subject of many theses, in Turin too. Ariodante Marianni brought out a translation in 1965 with Mondadori, and perhaps the most authoritative scholar has been Mario Praz who in 1975 made a short but deep study of Dylan's poetry pointing out his technical ability and affinities with surrealism, quoting a letter of Dylan's to Henry Treece, in which Dylan expatiates on his theory of poetry,..."I let an image "create" itself in my feelings..." Praz himself defines Dylan's poetry as "...verbal phonic magic, spiralling infinitely..."

Interest is still alive as *Under Milk Wood* was translated in 1991 for theatrical performance. It was first published in *Botteghe Oscure* in Rome by Marguerite Caetani in the Fifties.

Self-Violence in the Art of Muriel Spark

– *Therefore I lie with her, and she with me*
And in our faults by lies we flattered be
Shakespeare, Sonnet 138

Muriel Spark is one of the most interesting contemporary British authors in England today. She has written novels, short stories, poetry and criticism, and has won international prizes – the Italia prize, the James Tait Black Memorial Prize. It is worth noting that she became a Roman Catholic in 1954, and this could be at the basis of her interest in metaphysical problems, as religion in one way or another comes into her writing, i.e. *The Only Problem*, written in 1984 is a recent novel on the theme of patience, based on the biblical story of Job.

The Driver's Seat was first published in 1970 (later a film by F. Rossellini and G. Patroni Griffi) and has the power of a first-class piece of writing, a text with a plurality of interpretations, a 'readerly' text. The above quotation from Shakespeare's sonnet summarises the main theme of Muriel Spark's novel, *The Driver's Seat*, if we take the name of the protagonist Lise to be a pun, that as 'lies' it sums up her personality at actional and ontological levels. The meaning of Shakespeare's sonnet can be quoted as reference to how Lise sees herself and how she lives out the the inner part of her life, her alter ego, the part she fantasises for herself and which becomes a tragic and hallucinating reality for her, attracted irresistibly by the image and pattern of life she creates for herself as a modern independent young woman. Muriel Spark in this way deconstructs the myth of the good life based on a romantic attitude towards love, represented here in Lise as egoistic self-indulgence, self-love which turns inevitably into self-hate.

The 'deconstructive' approach that Muriel Spark has to her writing is evident by the way it lends itself to the Barthian type of structural analysis of the codes of interpretation, of the different voices which constitute the volume of the stereophony of the text, and also evokes the history of the change in presentation of character in the 19th and 20th century novel pinpointed by W.J. Harvey[1]:

> ...the novel in the 19th and 20th centuries, with its 'intrinsic' or internal presentation of character, encourages (the "assumption that moral discussions may take place in some inner free forum of the mind") this notion of subjectivity of the self as the "secret central ego lurking behind a gallery of social personae" and even as possessing "a heart of darkness in the character, a central mystery which is never quite presented.

The modern psychological concept of character which Lise embodies shows the technical dexterity of the writer who wishes to give a definite unequivocal stylistic cut to her work. Lise is a contemporary no nonsense individualist who knows what's what. There is a definitely ethical shape to her personality; and her very independence leads her to rebel against the various social roles she has been filling in society, as a not- so-young bachelor girl who works in an office. Her type of rebellion against society can be expressed through the words of William Frankena[2].

He argues quite perspicaciously, that although morality may be a 'social enterprise' which exists before the individual and thus is 'social in its origins', ethical concerns can only arise when 'we can think for ourselves' and achieve 'autonomy as moral agents' (i.e. modern emancipation). The rules of society are thus 'so internalised that we can be said to be inner-directed, to the stage, in which we think of ourselves in critical and general terms.' We become autonomous beings, who may refuse 'other-direction' by society for distinctively moral reasons.

This recalls

> the Kantian assertion that the basis of the moral law is to be found in the subject as capable of autonomous will and concentrates on the moral thinking of the individual as isolated, rational and capable of asking what is right or ought to be done."[3]

1. W.J. Harvey, *Character and the Novel*, London 1965.
2. William Frankena, *Ethics*, Englewood Cliffs 1963.
3. Cf. Michael Sandel, *Liberalism and the Limits of Justice*, Cambridge 1982.

The type of rebellion presented by Muriel Spark has a moral concern, reflected in the thoughts and actions of Lise. Lise, at a terrible critical moment in her life, does not indulge in self-pity except in an angry indirect way, in fact at a conscious level she refuses pity and help – a hard modern personality, and it does seem that Muriel Spark is concerned to be as objective and unemotional as possible in her writing – the anti-pathos presented is typically 'deconstructionist'. The critic Geoffrey Hartman, when talking about the phenomenological critics, Derrida, de Man and Hillis Miller (now a deconstructionist), who take their basic theoretical starting point from Nietzsche, states that they agree with him when he says "the deepest pathos is still aesthetic play". For them, the ethos of literature is not dissociable from its pathos, whereas for deconstructionist criticism, literature is precisely "that use of language which can purge pathos, which can show that it too is figurative, ironic or aesthetic."[4] At this point what is deconstruction could be the question, and again a quotation from Howard Felperin might serve: "it is a counter-enactment".

Placing Muriel Spark's art in a historical perspective we might see it as coming after the existentialist phase of modern romantic literature, an attempt to to get away from feeling, an exercise in classical restraint, precision and depth in presentation.

Lise's struggle becomes a great trial of strength, a fight against a mysterious inner force: it has a Promethean shading, supported by her proud character. Byron in his 'Prometheus' lists out the consistency of this spiritual battle:

> Like thee, Man is in part divine,
> A troubled stream from a pure source;
> And Man in portions can foresee
> His own funereal destiny;
> His wretchedness, and his resistance,
> And his sad unallied existence:
> To which his Spirit may oppose
> Itself – an equal to all woes-

4. Howard Felperin, *Beyond Deconstruction*, Oxford 1985 p.121.

And a firm will, and a deep sense,
Which even in torture can descry
Its own concentrated recompense,
Triumphant where it dares defy,
And making Death a Victory.

(Poems of July-September, 1816.)

For the Romantic Byron the struggle is heroic; for Muriel Spark, Lise is an anti-heroine, for she dies in vain, for a vain purpose.

The text as a stereophony of voices has been mentioned above, and Lise is presented on many levels of 'reality': but the main impression is one of a woman suffering from a deep-rooted neurosis, a 'sick' woman who externalises her subconscious suffering with bouts of hysteria: The novel covers a few days, the final crisis, the resolution of the 'unbalance' in Lise's life.

As Muriel Spark so aptly defines this novel enigmatically as... "it's a whydunnit in q-sharp major" and it has a message, this article could take this definition as a starting point. The message is manifold, on a literary level it's a sign that Muriel Spark does not want to be identified with latter day literature, such as the romantic existentialist novel – it is perhaps definable as a classical existentialist novel in the sense that the approach is objective – a neo-realistic sequence of events on the surface.

She then proceeds to deconstruct the traditional elements of the modern novel and its ingredients at a series of levels, the psychology of the identity of the one and only main character, closely observed during her few days' final movements, the questioning of modern myths, religions, metaphysics and the spirit of the age in a series of dramatic moments of suspense, enigma, horror, climaxes and a powerful horrific dénouement, mixing the plausible with the implausible, in a modernist parody of modern 'people' who appear on the scenes of the novel: in her own words it's a "whydunnit" and the reader led on by suspense, surprise, horror and the morbid fascination of the death of a young woman who wants to die, preferably by the hand of another, an ex-sexual maniac, is absorbed in the narrative right up to the final word. We are in the presence of an authentic work of art. At linguistic level[5] with reference to Muriel Spark we might say she is using "a rhetoric of difference, deferral, indirection and counter-enactment" and "the poetics of counter-enactment also has its master-trope, its chief figure, the very opposite of onomatopœia, the 'new-namer', and that figure is paranomasia, in Puttenham's scheme, 'the nicknamer', or as isbetter known to us, word-play, pun, or quibble".

Examining closely the title and other word phrases in the book we could read more deeply into the work. Is the "driver's seat" equal to the force which is at the basis of action. To be in the driver's seat is to lead others, and so an indirect indication of the main theme, rebellion against life guided from the outside, from above. Lise wants to drive her own life, in fact through to death, usurping a power which should not be wielded by her.

A hilarious use of the trope is to be found the episodc with Bill, the health fanatic, who is starting a youth movement called Yin-Yang Young, based on macrobiotics, and says

> On this diet the Regional Master for Northern Europe recommends one orgasm a day. At least. In the Mediterranean countries we are still researching that aspect.

But literary criticism is engaged in the "howdunnit" side of the matter. And I should like to point out the words of Nietzsche, as an indirect inspirer of post-modernism and deconstruction in literary criticism.

> It is not difficult to demonstrate that what is called 'rhetorical', as the devices of a conscious art, is present as a device of unconscious art in language and its development...... No such thing as an unrhetorical, 'natural' language exists that could be used as a point of reference: language itself is the result of purely rhetorical tricks and devices... Language is rhetoric for it only intends to convey a doxa (opinion), not an episteme (truth)... Tropes are not something that can be added or subtracted at will from language; they are its truest nature. There is no such thing as a proper meaning that can be

5. Cf. Felperin, *Op. Cit.*, p.185.

6. Quoted in Paul de Man, *Allegories of Reading* pp.105-6.

> communicated only in certain particular cases.[6]

This quotation from Paul de Man's book is Nietzsche's contribution to the deconstruction of philosophical truth, and is pertinent to existential literature and contemporary literary criticism. To go on, in a foreword to Carol Jacob's *The Dissimulating Harmony* (1978), Paul de Man distinguishes between methods of reading which simplify, omit difficulties, and, in effect paraphrase, and a 'genuinely analytical reading' or deconstruction which follows an argument. Deconstruction

> has the sequential coherence we associate with a demonstration or a particularly compelling narrative. But what is being compellingly told is precisely the loss of an illusory sequence.

The question is whether meaning should be integral to understanding at all costs, or whether it should

> be allowed to disintegrate under the negative elements in a text, however marginal or apparently trivial, that can only be silenced by suppression.

According to de Man, a rigorous analytical reading will demonstrate

> the necessary occurrence of this disruption....Reading becomes a parable (Gleichnis), an allegory of reading as the literal designation of its undoing:

This disruption of meaning

> occurs when the literal or figural status of the text's central event (its understanding) has to be, and cannot be, decided.

And this is precisely the reason for Muriel Spark's definition of her work as a "whydunnit", in which the 'central event' is the baffling enigma of Lise's desired death by the hand of another person, the final event in the final pages of the novel.

Muriel Spark's novel is a consummate parody – of romantic existential literature, of the modern identity of the independent woman, of objective truth, and the illusions of subjective truths, a profound study of modern neuroses, a 'sick' novel. She presents Lise, a young woman approaching middle age, sick of being alone, sick of sex and the impossibility of love, engaged on the everlasting search for identity, and sick now of the personality she perceives she has created for herself – efficient in life, the commanding person in the office, used to selecting her environment and her friends – men and women. The confusion which reigns in her inner self is epitomised in an incident in the taxi with Bill whom she has met casually on the plane:

> "You've got me for the next few days if you like," Bill says.... "You can't go on the bus crying like that. I don't get it. I can give you what you want, wait and see."

In the taxi she laughs harshly when Bill tries to kiss her. Then she lets him kiss her, emerging from the contact with raised eyebrows as who should say, 'What next?' 'I'm your type,' Bill says.

Her spiritual crisis explodes into episodes of hysteria, now more or less uncontrollable, and thus Muriel Spark brings up many modern beliefs and myths, question of identity, Narcissism, loneliness, the new fads and religions, and parodies such practices as macrobiological diets and health disciplines, modern eroticism, modern myths about Love, using as main theme a study of split personality, the schizophrenia of Lise "come viaggio nell'interiorità" ("a journey into the deep personality" (subconscious).[7]

Muriel Spark builds an identikit of Lise through visual details, 'short back/sides hair, styled high, 29 or 36,' 'dull blue-grey eyes', 'lips a straight line', 'nose short and wide','not good or bad-looking.' However the emphasis is on Lise's inner crisis, and these 'episodes' have a cumulative effect, achieving the immediacy of actuality. Lise is the chief actor in her own comedy, she chooses to be misinterpreted, to reveal her crisis, this race to self-destruction creates the suspense, the emotive tension of the novel, the logico-temporal order is disrupted to give preference to the inner psychological drama, the logic of the actional code is queried, and the enigma of why Lise is driven to want her own death is not answered directly, Muriel Spark is exploring the dark inner core of the psyche, a metaphysical questioning. The novel is the buildup of an

7. From a lecture by Joseph Campbell 'Myths for Living' *L'Espresso, Da Jung a Joyce di Elémire Zolla* n. 17, XXVI 29/4/90.

intense crisis, a self-indulgence of Lise who takes a sadomasochistic joy in externalising her tortured inner self. Early in the book, she turns on the salespeople of a shop she is going out of:

> At the door she turns to look back and says, with a look of satisfaction at her own dominance over the situation with an undoubtable excuse, 'I won't be insulted!'

The irreversibility of Lise's actions creates one of the fundamental ingredients of the novel-suspense.

As Barthes writes in *Valdemar*, the several codes detected in a text do not point out a 'true' one; the opposition of indeterminations and determinations creates 'signifiance", an undecidability becomes a condition of our reading... with the final effect of a "feeling of déjà lu, déjà fait": the codes are "a mirage of structures".

At a psychological level Lise has a power complex. She wishes to have the right to dispose of her life, desiring death and arranging it in her own way: maybe it is a reaction against the life she leads; the image of herself as she has created it. She often abstracts herself

> solemn, staring, (she sees) beyond the door (of her bed-sitter), meticulously neat, one-room flat... .....The lines of the room are pure; space is used as a pattern in itself, circumscribed by the dexterous pinewood outlines that ensued from the designer's ingenuity and austere taste when he was young, unknown, studious and strict-principled.

Another aspect of this plane of writing, the revelation of Lise's psyche is the disruption of the chronological sequence as an important technique in the process of the novel – a dramatisation achieved by flashbacks (Lise's office-life) and flash-forwards (the death of Lise, the police interrogation of the killer), which are outside the 'real' time of the novel.

Of course the novel runs very well at a visual 'realistic' level. The irreversibility of Lise's actions creates one of the fundamental ingredients of the whydunnit-suspense level. Muriel Spark describes the care that Lise takes over her dress, her punctiliousness, her fashionable bachelor's flat which she leaves behind her in the North of England to go on her (final) holiday to a hot seaside town in the south of Italy, her intellig-ence – Lise speaks four languages (dies speaking them!), her snobbishness (she dislikes the latest fashions, hippiness and untidiness), her determination and superiority in dealing with other people, whatever their social status, her self-criticism – she cries over her past life – she is at the end of her tether – her life is 'false' to her (cf. double meaning in her name Lise=lies) her rebellion against her predicament, (she chooses her death) seems to cry out against a normal human destiny. On a purely visual level, Muriel Spark puts us in Lise's place, the descript-ion of places is meticulous, and, uncannily, we seem to be a part of Lise herself on her holiday abroad.

However the opposite side to this realism is the dexterous use of language to express the inside of Lise's personality, her reactions, her decisions, the schizophrenic quality of her ex-istence. The tropes, the rhetoric and the imagery at the level of fantasy, the semic code reveals the poetry in the art of Muriel Spark.

An example of how wordplay effectively reveals the despair of Lise's alienated existence is shown when Lise talks about meeting the man she is looking for. Mrs. Fiedke, her friend she meets on holiday in Italy, recommends Richard, her nephew,

> "...that poor Richard may be the very man you're looking for."
> "Well, it's your idea," says Lise, "not mine. I wouldn't know till I'd seen him. Myself, I think he's round the corner somewhere, now, any time."
> "Which corner?" The old lady looks up and down the street which runs below them at the bottom of the steps.
> '"Any corner. Any old corner."
> '"Will you feel a presence? Is that how you'll know?"
> '"Not really a presence," Lise says. "The lack of an absence, that's what it is. I know I'll find it. I keep on making mistakes, though." She starts to cry...

To take another instance of Lise's interior instability; before going on holiday, Lise goes into a department store to buy a dress, there is a cumulative effect of hysteria through action and words:

> "That's my dress...It's a good fit. Lovely colours."
> "Doesn't stain."

> "Doesn't stain?"
> The customer (Lise) has flung the dress aside
> The salesgirl shouts, as if to assist her explanation.
> "Specially treated fabric...If you spill like a drop of sherry you just wipe it off. Look, Miss, you're tearing the neck."
> '"Do you think I spill things on my clothes?" the customer shrieks.
> '"Do I look as if I don't eat properly?..."

Hypersensitivity, class consciousness, alienation, all these psychological notations are at the root of this outburst. Lise reacts to being identified as being working class like the shop girl. She hates to be involved in friendly contact. Her negative attitude will culminate in self-hatred.

Chapter 3 begins with the horrific enunciation of Lise's demise:

> She will be found tomorrow morning dead from multiple stab-wounds...

This information is given before Lise's actual departure from England. This anticipation of the end of the novel creates the ground for suspense, how will it happen, and above all why this death. The mystery, the enigma is played upon and developed in a brilliant artefact of supreme technical accomplishment. The reader is tempted to analyse the whole text *à la* Barthes, that is, divide it into lexias, and codify each statement to reveal its complexity and depth ("The code is a perspective of quotations, a mirage of structures," – Barthes) to reach the 'signifiance', that is the complex plurality of the text, its volume, its stereography. (Cf. textual analysis of Poe's *Valdemar*). The dominating emotion called up by Muriel Spark is dismay and horror, the reader is involved in Lise's self-revelation, her antipathy for her life, and her self-hatred, her horrible egoism, her desperate pride which leads her to want to have it over and done with, as she has come to the end of her tether, her time has run out. And feels the horror of the waste of her life, she decides she will die, and with a supreme twist of black humour she will get somebody to kill her: her victim will be a rehabilitated sexual maniac whose killer instincts she recognises and reawakens. Her demonic plan which succeeds is her final rebellion against herself, the society which cannot give her what she wants, and her inner controlling force which keeps her 'sane' and 'ordinary' is liberated. She can't love or be loved, so she embraces self-hatred, death and darkness.

The story is certainly original and reading it is compulsive, as the text is rich, pertinent and dynamic. It has ecological tones too; here in this story of modern life, even nature has been den- ied and suppressed, in Lise's natural better self, and in the surroundings:

> The tall swaying pines among the litter of cones on the forest floor have been subdued into silence and into obedient hulks.

The imagery Muriel Spark uses has its force and appropriateness: Lise's self-repression can be noted in many accurate descriptions. She has: 'a detail-warden of a mouth'; 'a final-judging mouth'; her voice has: 'a little-girl tone'.

The theme is an horrific death, but it would be wrong to give the impression that there are no laughs to be had from the text, the humour is often extended and exaggerated to a peak of black humour, where one laughs or smiles in order not to cry out from shock and horror. An example of light humorous narrative: Lise is in a department store in a seaside town in Italy, where she has met an old-age pensioner on holiday, Mrs. Fiedke: (Lise is looking for a man who will be attracted by her, and who will be guided by her to kill her)

> Mrs. Fiedke started to scan the passers-by.
> "Would that be him, do you think? He looks very gaily dressed like yourself."
> "No, that's not him."
> "It's quite a problem, with all this choice. What about this one? No this one, I mean, crossing in front of that car? Would he be too fat?"
> "No, it isn't him"
> "It's very difficult, my dear, if you don't know the cast of person."
> "He could be driving a car," Lise had said...
> They go up, now to the third floor..."Not a great many gentlemen," Mrs. Fiedke remarks, "I doubt if you'll find your friend here."
> "I doubt it too," says Lise. "Although there are quite a few men employed here, aren't there?"
> "Oh, would he be a shop assistant?" Mrs. Fiedke says.
> "It depends," says Lise
> "These days," says Mrs. Fiedke.

The humour is light on the surface, Mrs.Fiedke does not know Lise's intentions, as the reader does. This knowledge, that Lise is looking for a potential sex maniac who could kill her makes the irony intense, the humour black. The novel is a series of frames, many of which are frankly humorous, in a light manner as becomes the holiday scene. However the tropes introduced are often more incisive, viz. sarcasm, irony. Lise very rarely refrains from making sarcastic remarks in her everyday exchanges with people: she is frankly rude to people who a few minutes or even seconds before were completely unknown to her. Her aggressive attitude towards life is symptomatic of her deep-rooted crisis, her repressed hysteria. Irony on the other hand is at the base of the main theme: Lise young and free, an emancipated modern girl with no one in this world to account to, desires death not love. She has exhausted her modest supply of grace, she cannot love anymore: an over self-absorbed woman, her almost biblical sense of self-righteousness leads her to an arrogant thirst for justice, to the point of intolerance. She becomes isolated and antisocial, her spiritual quest leads her not to grace but to darkness (the archetypal instance could be seen formulated in Proverbs 12, where justice is contrasted to wickedness). The deep tragedy of modern life is shown in one of its aspects in this very readable novel of Muriel Spark's. In the very moment of death, she reserves a revelatory climax: Lise does not achieve the liberation she has planned for:

> As the knife descends to her throat she screams, evidently perceiving how final is finality.

And the author's final comment on the ordinariness and banality of everyday life tones down the high emotion of the horrific end of Lise to a universal human truth:

> He sees already the gleaming buttons of the policeman's uniform, hears the cold and the confiding, the hot and the barking voices, sees already the holsters and epaulets and all those trappings devised to protect them from the indecent exposure of fear and pity, pity and fear.

This is the killer's anticipation of the immediate future. This flash-forward ends the novel.

I Temi Religiosi nella Poesia di T.S.Eliot

Scrivendo della connessione tra religione e poesia T.S.Eliot mise in evidenza fin dall'inizio un elemento per lui fondamentale: il problema del credere. A questo proposito, nel gennaio del 1927 egli pubblicú sulla rivista *The Enemy* un articolo da cui emerge chiara la sua analisi del problema:

> Io non credo che la poesia si possa mai separare da qualcosa che io chiamerei il credere e al quale non vedo alcuna ragione per negare il nome di fede a meno che non si vogliano rimescolare i termini. Non dovrebbe quasi essere necessario dire che non sarà inevitabilmente una ortodossa fede cristiana, sebbene si possa affermare questa possibilità dato che il cristianesimo probabilmente continuerà a modificarsi, come è già avvenuto in passato, in qualcosa in cui si puó credere (e non mi riferisco a modificazioni consapevoli come il modernismo ecc... che hanno sempre l'effetto opposto). La maggior parte delle persone vive al di sotto del livello del credere o del dubbio. Ci vuole applicazione e una specie di genio e credere in "Qualsiasi cosa" (e non intendo semplicemente il credere in qualche religione) diventerà probabilmente man mano piú difficile con il passare del tempo.

Come scrisse Leavis (il famoso critico e commentatore di Cambridge) "il signor Eliot ha una preoccupazione specificatamente religiosa", nell'esaminare la quale possiamo prendere come punto di partenza proprio questa sua idea di fede, la necessità di un credo convinto, di una fede solida, che ritorna nelle sue poesie come parte dell'affermarsi dell'interesse religioso.

Prima di continuare è peró opportuno notare come il passo sopra citato fu scritto da Eliot al tempo della sua adesione formale alla Chiesa Anglo Cattolica e cioè precisamente nel 1927, è infatti da quel momento in poi che la religione diventa uno dei principali interessi della sua poesia.

Nel suo dramma *La Rocca* egli puntualizza una serie intera di temi religiosi. Il credere viene esplicitamente menzionato nel Coro VIII:

> "Peró niente è impossibile, niente,
> a uomini di fede e convinzione."

Il lato opposto di questa fede è certamente il dubbio, il dubbio e il timore di un tradimento interiore che assale il poeta in una grande poesia del 1930, il *Mercoledi' delle ceneri*. Nella quinta sezione di quest' opera i dubbi e le interrogazioni a se stesso appaiono evidenti. La certezza della fede che noi incontriamo nella poesia di Dante, fonte di ispirazione di tanta poesia eliotiana, viene a mancare. Incertezze e difficoltà, confermate dall' ambiguità dei termini usati, invadono il poeta:

Se la parola perduta è perduta, se la parola spesa è spesa
Se la parola non detta e non udita
E' non udita e non detta
sempre è la parola non detta, il Verbo non udito,
Il Verbo senza parola, il Verbo
nel mondo e per il mondo;
e la luce brilló nelle tenebre e
il mondo inquieto contro il Verbo ancora
ruotava attorno al centro del Verbo silenzioso".

In alcuni momenti del testo il significato mistico che viene attribuito da Eliot al movimento e alla vita sulla terra è evidente. Nel viaggio spirituale del poeta la fede diventa piú forte e allo stesso tempo piú difficile da comprendere:

....vi è ancora fede
ma la fede e l'amore e la speranza sono
nell'attendere".

Nell'ultimo gruppo di poesie chiamato *Little Gidding*, un paesino nella contea di Cambridge dove Nicholas Ferrar fondó nel Seicento una comunità di suore anglicane, la fede equivale alla disciplina, essa diventa ordine, accettazione, o meglio volontà tesa alla preghiera, fede e preghiera che sono, nell' opera di T.S.Eliot, strettamente legate fra di loro:

Se tu passassi da qui
prendendo qualsiasi strada...
sarebbe sempre lo stesso...
Sei qui per inginocchiarti
dove la preghiera è stata valida. Una preghiera è piú
che un ordine di parole... la comunicazione
dei morti ha lingue di fuoco oltre il linguaggio dei vivi.

Dimostrato l'interesse e la presenza costante del tema religioso nell'opera di Eliot la domanda a cui vogliamo rispondere è: qual è la strada che conduce la sua poesia a quella che potremmo definire, citando Matthew Arnold, "alta serietà" e come arriva egli a decidere che la religione e specificatamente la religione cattolica, che egli considerava come la piú profonda espressione dello spirito dell'uomo in armonia con Dio, rappresenta la strada che intende seguire? Per rispondere a queste domande si rende necessario ripercorrere rapidamente le prime poesie di Eliot e in particolare: *Prufrock e altre osservazioni* la sua prima collezione del 1917. In queste poesie giovanili Eliot scrive di un taedium vitae e di una accidia spirituale che pervade di sé il suo atteggiamento verso la vita:

> Ho misurato la mia vita con cucchiaini da caffè.

Questo malessere, quest'inedia quasi baudelairiana, riappaiono nelle poesie successive attraverso personaggi diversi. In *Ritratto di una signora* egli racconta la vita della donna come una sorta di incubo vissuto nell'estranazione ed alienazione dell'assoluta mancanza di contatti umani.

> Senza queste amicizie – che 'cauchemar' la vita!"

Anche nei *Preludi*, nei quali Eliot analizza la propria depressione e il venir meno del suo spirito, prevale il senso di soffocamento spirituale reso tecnicamente attraverso l'effetto "collage": la transizione da un livello psicologico all' altro, la mobilità della prospettiva, dalla seconda alla terza alla prima persona, la descrizione di cose indescrivibili. Tutto è in contrapposizione, l'anima in pena e la beffa, lo spirito sofferente schernito dal commento volgare e il finale che accenna all'incompatibilità di livelli di vita diversi:

> Le mille immagini sordide
> di cui era composta la tua anima...
> Avevi una visione della strada
> che a stento la strada comprende...
> La sua anima si tendeva nei cieli...
> Io sono spinto da fantasie che s'attorcono
> attorno a queste immagini e s'attardano:
> la nozione di qualcosa che è infinitamente
> dolce e infinatamente soffre.
> Strofinatevi la mano sulla bocca e ridete
> i mondi ruotano come antiche donne
> che raccolgono legna in lotti da vendere.

Il movimento in avanti della coscienza di Eliot passa attraverso la memoria, una componente importante dello spirito:

La Memoria!
Hai la chiave.
(da *Rapsodia di una notte di vento*)

In *Gerontion*, 1920, si notano elementi di movimento spirituale piú positivi. Qualcosa al di fuori del poeta, segni e valori oggettivi, viene a formare la muscolatura della poesia. Per la maggior parte della gente vi è una realtà spirituale dietro le apparenze:

Eccomi qui, vecchio, in un mese arido...
aspettando
la pioggia...".

I segni sono presi per miracoli:

Vogliamo vedere un segno!
.....Nell'adolescenza dell' anno
Venne Cristo la tigre...

L'aridità dello spirito qui evocata e ripresa nella grande poesia del 1922 *La terra desolata* è in parte compensata dai versi associati con misteri religiosi; nella *Terra desolata* la risoluzione è ironica, la poesia finisce con le parole sanscrite Shantih, shantih, shantih, versi mistici orientali, che Eliot traduce dall' Upanishad con "la pace che oltrepassa ogni comprensione".

Nella sua rivista *Criterion* del gennaio 1926 Eliot si associa ad "una tendenza, distinguibile anche nell' arte, orientata verso una concezione piú profonda della Ragione". Su questa stessa rivista, scrivendo dello scrittore francese Proust, egli ne parla come di un "punto di demarcazione tra una generazione per la quale la dissoluzione del valore aveva un valore positivo in se stesso e la generazione la quale inizia a volgere la sua attenzione ad una formazione dell' anima severa ed ascetica, una sorta di atletismo analogo alla preparazione fisica di un corridore".

Alla ricerca di una ideale preparazione spirituale dopo la descrizione della decadenza della vita cittadina moderna e l'insistenza sui valori materiali nel mondo contemporaneo, nella poesia *Bisbigli di immortalità* del 1920 Eliot evince un fatto incontrovertibile nella vita di tutto il creato e dell'uomo in particolare: l'inevitabilità della morte.

Evocato nella poesia, prima con un riferimento al drammaturgo elisabettiano John Webster e poi a John Donne, diacono della cattedrale di S. Paolo a Londra, il tema della morte come punto di partenza per la vita immortale sarà ripetuto insistentemente nel III coro de *La rocca*:

Potete eludere la Vita, ma non la Morte
Non potrai negare lo Sconosciuto.

Questi versi, nei quali lo Sconosciuto è identificabile con Cristo, introducono un altro tema religioso importante che apparirà spesso nei lavori di Eliot, dove Cristo, la cui immagine segna i punti salienti della poesia eliotiana, appare come mediatore tra la vita mortale e la vita immortale.

Ne *La rocca* alla figura di Cristo viene data piú vasta risonanza attraverso una dichiarazione diretta:

E il figlio dell' uomo non fu crocefisso una volta per tutte,
il sangue dei martiri non fu versato una volta per tutte,
le vite dei Santi non vennero donate una volta per tutte:
e vi saranno sempre Martiri e Santi.

La figura di Cristo viene introdotta per la prima volta ne *La terra desolata*:

Chi è quel terzo che sempre ti cammina accanto?

come una presenza misteriosa che ci accompagna sempre.

In *Una canzone per Simeone* che fa parte del gruppo di poesie *Ariel* i tre temi della Morte, della figura di Cristo Figlio e della Preghiera si intersecano in un movimento positivo teso alla ricerca del significato della disciplina spirituale:

Possa il Figliolo, il Verbo non pronunciante e impronunciato ancora,
accordare la consolazione d' Israele
a un uomo di ottant' anni e che non ha domani.

La morte e con essa la strada dell' immortalità erano già state invocate ne *Il viaggio dei Magi* dove i tre re riconoscono nella nascita divina un evento che avrebbe cambiato la loro vita. L'evidenza storica, la storia vera composta di fatti che sono alla base della religione cristiana diventano componente essenziale del testo:

Vi fu una Nascita, certo,
ne avemmo prova e non avemmo dubbio. Avevo visto nascita e morte.
Ma le avevo pensate differenti; per noi questa Nascita fu
come un'aspra ed amara sofferenza, come la Morte, la nostra morte.
Tornammo ai nostri luoghi, ai nostri Regni,
ma ormai non piú tranquilli, nelle antiche leggi,
fra un popolo straniero che è rimasto aggrappato ai propri idoli.
Io sarei lieto di un' altra morte.

In un' altra poesia, *Marina*, il tema della morte ha un contrario; la morte diventa infatti punto di partenza per una vita nuova (il riferimento è a *La Vita Nuova* di Dante).

Nella poesia di Eliot vi sono immagini di speranza; la figlia Marina è dispersa, ma poi ritrovata, le immagini di morte sono sconfitte dalle immagini di vita eterna; le acque del mare diventano simboli di un viaggio dello spirito nell'ignoto, nella nuova vita spirituale:

... potessi
Rimettere la mia vita per questa vita,
la mia parola per ció che non è detto
il risvegliato,le labbra aperte, la speranza, i bastimenti".

L' analisi dei testi sino a qui citati e l'esame della ricerca religiosa di Eliot confermano come la poesia rappresenti per l'autore una sorta di viaggio spirituale.

La sua poesia è rappresentazione della coscienza, la consapevolezza del pensiero occidentale, l' universalità della tradizione cristiana e l'attualità della chiesa cattolica presentate globalmente come momenti nella propria vita poetica.

La nostra lettura segue un corso obbligato e la poesia, come lo stesso Eliot dichiara nel passo citato all'inizio di questo saggio, è contenuta nella fede del poeta.

La poesia ha la sua magia, è il suo miracolo ed il lettore partecipa ad essa, cosi' come afferma Coleridge, con "la sospensione del dubbio".

La consapevolezza, la coscienza e una attività fuori dal Tempo si presentano con la realtà senza Tempo.

La poesia *La Funzione della Domenica mattina* ci dà l'affermazione di una realtà quotidiana :

In principio era il Verbo
superfetazione di tó én.

Per Eliot la poesia è una preparazione al progressivo raggiungimento dell'espressione religiosa cristiana. La realtà superiore dello spirito sempiterno è una esperienza personale. Eliot poeta fa poesia, la poesia traccia il movimento dell'esperienza religiosa e l'esperienza diventa immagine. Leggiamo una poesia del 1932 il *Mercoledi' delle Ceneri* che all'inizio richiama i versi del poeta italiano del Duecento Guido Cavalcanti:

Perch'I' no spero di tornar giammai.

(Because I do not hope to turn again)
(Perch'io non spero piú di tornare)

In questi versi Eliot, alla ricerca di una vita nuova, rinuncia alla vita passata.

La lotta dello spirito è peró insopportabile per l'umanità e di conseguenza il pocta "grida" invocando la salvezza e pregando affinché lo sforzo non sia insopportabile:

Insegnaci ad aver cura e a non curare
e in finale il grido, la preghiera piena
d'angoscia e sofferenza :
Sorella benedetta, santa madre, spirito
della fonte, spirito del giardino
... non sopportare che io sia separato
e a Te giunga il mio grido "

La poesia di Eliot è caratterizzata da una specie di circolarità, un movimento di ritorno dei molti temi che egli affronta.

La sua ultima grande incomparabile poesia *I Quattro quartetti* è un intreccio di temi di meditazione religiosa.
La prima delle quattro poesie della raccolta, *Burnt Norton*, presenta costante il tentativo di puntualizzare una realtà sovrannaturale:

la specie umana
non sopporta troppa realtà
Ma lo spirito è nella vita dell'uomo una presenza
costante che pervade di se la vita di tutti noi.

E' un paradosso: l'immobilità nel movimento, "erhebung" senza moto come dice lo stesso Eliot (erhebung significa elevazione).

La permanenza dello spirito si rivela:

> L' immobilità di un vaso cinese pur
> si muove perpetuamente nella sua immobilità

L'eternità nell'esistenza stessa, l'apparenza sempre mutevole di una realtà fissa:

> E tutto è sempre ora
> il dettaglio del disegno è movimento
> l'amore stesso è immobile

In *East Coker*, la seconda poesia dei *Quartetti*, Eliot ci descrive l'esperienza religiosa della vita eterna in un passo di poesia paradossale che ci addita la transizione mistica dall' esistenza temporale a quella eterna dello spirito:

> Per arrivare là
> per arrivare dove sei, per partire da dove non sei,
> devi passare per una via dove non c'è estasi.
> Per arrivare a ció che non sai
> devi passare per una via che è quella dell' ignoranza.
> Per possedere ció che non possiedi
> devi passare per la via della spogliazione.
> Per arrivare a ció che non sei.
> Devi andare per la via dove non sei.
> E quello che non sai è l'unica cosa che sai
> E quello che possiedi è quello che non possiedi
> E dove sei è dove non sei.

Questo brano, ricolmo di paradossi che anticipano e rispondono ai nostri dubbi ed interrogativi, diventa una introduzione alla sezione successiva che sviluppa i paradossi per presentare il rito, la religione, la realtà di Cristo, il suo significato come sacramento cristiano della Comunione. Nel paradosso della realtà, dove il mortale si congiunge con l'immortale, vi è un effetto di intensità barocca resa attraverso immagini orripilanti dove la malattia porta alla salute, dove il bisturi fa zampillare il sangue, ma risana, dove tutta l' umanità è ammalata, il mondo diventa un gigantesco ospedale e il sacramento rimane l'unica possibile salvezza. La festa cristiana del sacrificio di Cristo, il venerdi' santo, è il nostro riferimento:

Il sangue grondante la nostra unica bevanda
la carne sanguinosa il nostro unico cibo:
ció nonostante ci piace pensare
che siamo sani, di carne e sangue sostanziosi –
eppoi, nonostante questo, chiamiamo santo questo venerdi.

L' odissea spirituale del cristiano viene tracciata nella parte finale di questa poesia come una crisi di mezza età.
Nei primi versi de *La Divina Commedia* Dante esprime lo stesso turbamento:

Nel mezzo del cammin di nostra vita
mi ritrovai per una selva oscura
ché la dritta via era smarrita.

mentre nel romanzo *Little Dorrit* Charles Dickens ci propone il tema della stanchezza dello spirito attraverso il personaggio di Arthur Clennam:

So, here I am in the middle way...
(Cosi', eccomi al punto di metà strada...)

E cosa puó fare l'individuo che si sente perduto, colto dalla depressione? Cosi' risponde Eliot:

Per noi vi è solo il tentare. Il resto non è affar nostro.

In un brano della poesia....... Eliot descrive la vita dell' uomo, semplice e mortale:

Casa è il nostro punto di partenza. Man mano che invecchiamo
il mondo diventa piú strano,l'intreccio piú complicato
di morti e viventi. Non il momento intenso
isolato, senza prima o dopo,
ma una vita accesa in ogni momento
e non la vita di un uomo solo
ma di vecchie pietre che non possono essere decifrate.
Vi è un'ora per la sera sotto la luce stellare,
un'ora per la sera sotto la luce di lampade
(la sera con l'album delle fotografie).
L'amore è quasi sè stesso
Quando qui e ora cessano di significare.
I vecchi dovrebbero essere esploratori
qui o là non importano
Dobbiamo stare fermi muovendoci ancora

verso un'altra intensità
per un'ulteriore unione, una comunione piú profonda
attraverso il freddo oscuro e la desolazione vuota,
il grido dell'onda, il grido del vento, le acque sterminate
della procellaria e del delfino. Nella mia fine è il mio inizio.

La poesia diventa cosi' un resoconto del viaggio dell' uomo e dell' esperienza che lo conduce, attraverso l'oscurità e la morte, alla conquista dell' amore divino e della vita eterna.

Una poesia questa che viene proposta sul piano dell' esperienza mistica religiosa concretizzata mediante il linguaggio simbolico ed immaginoso, il pensiero e la sensibilità che sono la vita stessa per l' individuo, lo scrittore-poeta e il lettore-partecipante.

Nella terza poesia, *The Dry Salvages*, Eliot si avvicina ai temi religiosi in modo diverso, attraverso la rappresentazione della sofferenza dell' essere uomo e la necessità di abbracciare una disciplina spirituale. La poesia si apre con una immagine della religione primitiva.

Secondo T.S.Eliot, l' uomo, anche quello primitivo, non ha mai creduto alla mera materialità, ma in qualcosa che è dietro l' apparenza, un tentativo di oltrepassare la semplice fenomenalità e conquistare una realtà invisibile che puó dirci qualcosa e comunicare direttamente con noi:

Il mare ha molte voci
molti dei e molte voci
... il fiume è dentro a noi.

Il grande dio bruno del fiume rappresenta la coscienza interiorizzata dell' individuo. Anche l' uomo primitivo era consapevole della presenza dello spirito fuori e dentro se stesso.

Nella seconda parte della poesia l' autore si cimenta con i problemi spirituali. Si domanda il perché della sofferenza senza fine:

Dove è la fine di essa, l'ululo senza suono
l'appassire silenzioso dei fiori dell'autunno...

Dove è la fine per i rottami alla deriva,
la preghiera dell'osso sulla spiaggia, l'impregabile

preghiera all'annuncio calamitoso?

e giunge alla conclusione che l' unica strada possibile è l' accettazione della sofferenza e della morte, la rinuncia a ció che era certo nella vita.

Anni di vita tra il rottame
di ció in cui si credeva come il piú affidabile
e perció piú adatto alla rinuncia.

La vita , la nostra forza fisica ci mancheranno, taciamo e aspettiamo la morte inevitabile:

... l' innegabile
fragore della campana dell' ultima annunciazione

La fine della veglia spirituale è mistica. Il mistero della Morte e di Dio - la finalità come inizio, aspettando l' annuncio dell' eternità:

Non ve n'è fine, l'ululo senza voce,
dell' Annunciazione

La preghiera fa parte della disciplina spirituale. Come tema poetico è importante quanto la fede e riappare costantemente intrecciato ad essa attraverso l'invocazione a Maria, madre di Dio:

Signora il cui tabernacolo si erge sul promontorio
prega per tutti quelli che sono sulle navi,
...ripeti una preghiera anche per conto
delle donne che hanno visto figli e mariti
partire e non tornare.
Figlia del tuo figlio,
Regina del Cielo.

L' ultima sezione di *Dry Salvages* tenta di definire il momento eterno:

Ma per afferrare
il punto di intersezione dell'atemporale
con il tempo, è un'occupazione per un santo
Neanche occupazione, ma qualcosa data
e presa in una morte che dura una vita in amore,
ardore e altruismo e autorinuncia.

La poesia di Eliot ha molte qualità: l'enunciato filosofico del brano sopracitato puó deludere per la sua ovvietà categorica , ma il resto del brano ci dimostra come Eliot riesca a compiere una transizione magistrale, di grande potenza e profondità lirica, verso il mistico.

Per la maggior parte di noi, vi è solo il momento inatteso,
il momento dentro e fuori del tempo
il raptus della distrazione, perso in un raggio di sole,
il timo selvatico non visto, o il lampo invernale,
o la cascata, o musica sentita cosi'profondamente
che non è sentita affatto, ma sei la musica stessa
mentre dura la musica.

E' questo un momento di partecipazione dell' individuo ad una dimensione mistica che porta all'unione con Cristo. Il momento atemporale viene suggerito come possibile in un possibile tempo e luogo. Quello che è certo è il modo di vivere religioso. Questa è una certezza che puó essere afferrata e che conduce, attraverso l'esperienza mistica, alla liberazione dal tempo.

La poesia finale dei *Quattro quartetti* si intitola *Little Gidding*. Little Gidding è un piccolo paese nella contea di Cambridge dove un mistico, Nicholas Ferrar, fondó un convento trecento anni fa. Eliot, che ricorda questo episodio come un evento di grande importanza spirituale, plasma la sua poesia sui temi spirituali maturati in quel luogo tanti anni prima e ne fa ora motivi poetici propri: l' eternità, la fede, la ricerca, l' accettazione della preghiera, l' atemporalità dello spirito contrapposto allo sfacelo della civiltà, alla grettezza dell' umanità. In un brano che richiama Dante Eliot afferma che la meta ideale dello spirito, il quale sempre deve avere uno scopo, è il "raffinamento" , la comunicazione con l' ineffabile:

Se tu venissi da questa parte,
prendendo qualsiasi rotta, iniziando da qualsiasi punto
in qualsiasi momento o in qualsiasi stagione,
sarebbe sempre lo stesso: dovresti liberarti
dal senso e dalla nozione. Non sei qui per verificare
istruirti o informare la curiosità,
o fare rapporto. Sei qui per inginocchiarti
dove la preghiera è stata valida. E la preghiera è piú
che un ordine di parole, l'occupazione consapevole
della mente che prega o il suono della voce che prega
E quello che i morti non potevano dire quando erano in vita,

possono dirlo essendo morti: la comunicazione
dei morti ha lingue di fuoco al di là del linguaggio dei vivi.
Qui, l'intersezione del momento atemporale
è l' Inghilterra e nessun posto. Mai e sempre.

Lo spirito progredisce nelle nostre vite, ma il suo scopo è il rinnovamento, il recupero, il raffinamento dopo la ri-emanazione:

E infine il dolore lacerante della re-emanazione
di tutto ció che hai fatto, e stato;...
...Da un torto ad un altro lo spirito esarcebato
procede, a meno che ristabilito da quel fuoco raffinante
dove devi muoverti a tempo, come una ballerina.

Nella terza sezione di *Little Gidding*, dopo il brano di memoria dantesca, Eliot torna a parlare delle norme della vita spirituale, valuta la funzione dell' errore, della memoria, dell' amore e indirizza alla purificazione poiché dopo la preghiera la salvezza verrà:

Vi sono tre condizioni che spesso si rassomigliano
peró si differenziano completamente...
L'attaccamento a se stessi e alle cose e alle persone, distacco
da se stessi e dalle cose e dalle persone; e, crescendo tra di loro,
indifferenza
che rassomiglia agli altri come la morte rassomiglia alla vita....

L'errore umano ha la sua funzione, fa parte della natura umana decaduta; puó essere spiegato, cancellato per intercessione:

Il peccato è addicevole ma
tutto andrà bene,
e ogni specie di cose andrà bene.
Con la purificazione del motivo
nelle ragioni della nostra supplica.

Nella quinta sezione, l'ultimo di *Little Gidding*, Eliot rappresenta la circolarità paradossale della vita spirituale:

Ció che chiamiamo l'inizio è spesso la fine
e fare una fine è fare un inizio.
La fine è dove incominciamo.
... Moriamo con i morenti
... Siamo nati con i morti.

Cosi' la poesia sottolinea la scoperta e l' accettazione della nostra dimensione spirituale. L'esperienza poetica di Eliot si offre qui al lettore come invito a partecipare al riconoscimento dell'energia dello spirito che è la vita eterna anticipata dal mistero della religione, recupero, ripresa, rinnovo:

Con il disegnare di quest'Amore e la voce di questo Richiamo
non desisteremo dalla ricerca...
Subito ora, qui, ora, sempre
Una condizione di semplicità completa
(che costa meno di tutto)
E tutto andrà bene
e ogni specie di cosa andrà bene
quando le lingue di fiamma avvolte
nel nodo incoronato del fuoco
e il fuoco e la rosa sono uno.

I TRADUTTORI

Secondo alcuni famosi studiosi, quali Theodore Savory, tradurre un'arte, per altri, fra cui Eric Jacobsen, è un mestiere; altri ancora lo considerano una scienza. Sir Randolph Quirk afferma che tradurre "... è uno dei compiti piú difficili che uno scrittore possa intraprendere. L'idea che il tradurre implichi qualcosa in piú rispetto alla semplice conoscenza di due lingue è chiaramente affermata da Levy il quale a questo proposito dichiara:

> ... una traduzione non è una composizione monistica, ma una interpretazione e un conglomerato di due strutture. Da un lato vi è un contenuto semantico e l'insieme formale dell'originale, dall'altro l'intero sistema di caratteristiche estetiche legato alla lingua della traduzione.

Il processo che viene generalmente Definito 'traduzione' comporta la resa di un testo dalla lingua di partenza alla lingua d'arrivo per assicurare che il significato superficiale sia pressochè simile nelle due lingue e che le strutture della lingua siano conservate il piú possibile nella lingua d'arrivo senza distorsioni.

Già nel '700, Alexander Fraser Tytler nel suo saggio *I Principi della Traduzione* enunciava tre principi base secondo cui:

- la traduzione deve dare una trascrizione completa dell'idea dell'opera originale
- lo stile e il modo di scrivere debbono conservare lo stesso carattere dell'originale
- la traduzione deve possedere la disinvoltura della composizione originale.

La teoria di traduzione piú rigorosa è quella secondo cui il processo di traduzione coinvolge il trasferimento del 'significato' contenuto in una serie di segni linguistici in un'altra serie di segni linguistici tramite l'uso competente del dizionario e della grammatica. Oltre a ció, è comunque necessario ricordare che il processo coinvolge una vasta gamma di criteri linguistici non trascurabili. A questo proposito Edward Sapir asseriva che "la lingua è una guida alla realtà sociale ", che l'esperienza viene largamente determinata dalle abitudini linguistiche della comunità e che ogni struttura separata rappresenta una realtà separata. Juri Lotman afferma che la lingua "è un sistema per modellare " e che nessuna lingua puó esistere a meno che non sia intrisa nel contesto di una cultura, "cosicchè il traduttore che tratta il testo in isolamento lo fa a suo rischio e pericolo", mentre Roman Jacobson distingue tre tipi di traduzione:

- la traduzione intralingue o il rifacimento delle parole (l'interpretazione dei segni verbali attraverso altri segni nella stessa lingua)
- la traduzione interlingue o la traduzione vera e propria (l'interpretazione dei segni verbali per mezzo di qualche altra lingua)
- la traduzione intersemiotica o trasmutazione (l'interpretazione dei segni verbali tramite segni non verbali).

Il secondo tipo di traduzione, quella interlingue, è quella piú comunemente usata. Nell'analizzare questo tipo di traduzione è necessario sottolineare, come fa lo stesso Jacobson, che non vi è mai equivalenza completa fra duelingue, neppure nel caso della cosiddetta sinonimia. A conferma di questa affermazione possiamo citare alcun esempi.

Vediamo il caso del termine 'perfetto' per il quale i dizionari offrono il sinonimo 'ideale'. In realtà, pur essendo i due termini molto simili, non vi è una completa equivalenza poichè ogni unità contiene una serie di associazioni e connotazioni non trasferibili. In testi scientifici e tecnici il campo di associazioni è naturalmente molto piú ristretto rispetto a quello letterario, a cui si riferiscono in genere gli studiosi citati; ció nonostante la pluralità di sensi e significati rimane un problema, come del resto è un problema anche la traduzione di termini che rappresentano processi industriali nuovi o esempi di cultura e di istituzioni diversi. Ad esempio possiamo citare il termine inglese 'public school' che non indica la scuola pubblica statale, definita 'state school', ma un collegio-convitto tradizionale, costoso ed elitario.

Altro esempio interessante quello del termine italiano 'carosello' il quale non puó essere tradotto in inglese se non usando una parafrasi quale 'TV spot'. Questi semplici esempi a dimostrazione del fatto che il traduttore deve possedere una vasta cultura nelle lingue che usa.

Fino a quando si tratta di formule fisse e ampiamente conosciute come ad esempio "How do you do ?" - piacere- il compito del traduttore non presenta particolari difficoltà. Ma il suo lavoro, anche in campo tecnico od industriale, diventa difficile quando egli non conosce gli specifici processi di lavorazione del settore o l'attrezzatura che deve descrivere e gli stessi dizionari a volte deludono. Cito a questo riguardo un esempio tratto da un famoso dizionario tecnico che, in edizioni precedenti spiegava in modo corretto un termine usato in aeronautica, ma che, nelle sue edizioni successive ha creato un nonsenso, poichè il revisore non era a conoscenza del significato del termine inglese e ha cosi' omesso il riferimento al settore aeronautico. Si tratta di un grafico che riassume la situazione durante il volo di un aereo. Il grafico si chiama 'How goes it chart' dove "How goes it?" fa riferimento alla situazione di volo in tempo reale e viene tradotto 'tout court' come il grafico di Howgozit dove quest'ultimo termine è reso usando la maiuscola come se si trattasse di Newton o Galilei. Purtroppo si trovano, nella spiegazione dei termini, errori anche piú gravi, di grammatica; un esempio di questo è la voce 'adobe' che indica mattoni cotti al sole e viene tradotta in inglese come "mattoni cotti nel sole" - "bricks baked at the sun".

I dizionari possono essere di grande aiuto, sono anzi indispensabili, ma non sono infallibili dal momento che ogni parola cambia significato a seconda del contesto nel quale viene usata. E' inoltre necessario aggiungere che la lingua inglese ha la tendenza a sfruttare piú volte la stessa parola che puó quindi avere molteplici significati diversi; una parola semplice, estremamente comune puó infatti assumere significati nuovi ed inaspettati in settori diversi. Prendiamo ad esempio il termine 'off' che vediamo spesso comparire su apparecchi elettrici e che sappiamo significare: spento, interrotto. Lo stesso termine, usato in contesti diversi puó voler dire -finito, dietro le quinte, esterno, altro, libero, vuoto, senza impegni, esaurito, non piú fresco, stantio, lontano, distante, via, in partenza, da, non molto discosto da, di, con, indisposto; con certi verbi puó indicare rimozione o separazione, ad es. "Take off your coat" con altri ancora definisce il completamento di un'azione, 'Finish off,' 'pay off '. Questa esemplificazione dimostra chiaramente come il dizionario non possa essere usato alla cieca.

A questa difficoltà si aggiunge il grande problema della microlingua, la lingua specializzata, la lingua del settore o di una specialità che puó essere sconosciuta anche agli addetti ai lavori; esempi di microlingua sono il linguaggio della Borsa, della Sala Cambi, della Finanza, del settore assicurativo, dell' Informatica,linguaggi che si servono spesso di abbreviazioni che a loro volta diventano elementi di una nuova microlingua. Riporto a chiarimento un esempio del prof. Porcelli riguardante il famoso acronimo BBC usato in una pubblicità per computer, che nel contesto particolare in cui viene usato indica il micro-computer Acorn adottato dalla televisione di stato britannica e non si riferisce all'ente stesso.

Altro esempio è quello relativo al termine CAD inteso come Computer-Aided-Design , termine che, in questa accezione, non ha niente a che fare con il significato originario della parola che significa ' cialtrone, canaglia ' e qui non siamo a livello di comprensione delle parole in sè quanto piuttosto di conoscenza della realtà tecnologica o della teoria scientifica a cui i vocaboli fanno riferimento.

Cito ancora un esempio che fa riferimento alla terminologia del DP (data processing). In un glossario riguardante questo termine venivano date sei possibili traduzioni del termine inglese 'Clear' di cui tre come sostantivo (annullamento, azzeramento, scarico) e tre come verbo (azzerare, cancellare, scaricare) dove è interessante sottolineare il fatto che le diverse possibili varianti non rappresentano casi di sinonimia, ma indicano operazioni diverse.

La traduzione è stata a lungo considerata un'attività secondaria, un processo 'meccanico' piuttosto che 'creativo' in grado di essere esercitato da qualsiasi persona con una preparazione base in una lingua straniera; un'attività quindi di secondo grado la cui analisi sempre stata svolta sul prodotto invece che sul processo.

Se peró si riflette sulla quantità di testi letterari, scientifici e tecnici che vengono tradotti per essere utilizzati da studenti e professionisti, tecnici e scienziati, e piú in generale da tutti coloro che si occupano di traduzioni, non stupisce il fatto che sia stato recentemente avvertito il bisogno di studiare sistematicamente la traduzione, una necessità che sorge in relazione ai problemi direttamente connessi al processo stesso. Quando poi si pensa che la traduzione è diffusa soprattutto a livelli di cultura di massa, musica moderna popolare, cinema, teatro, televisione, sorge immediato il problema della 'valutazione'. Per analizzare questo problema è necessario premettere che non esiste un canone universale con cui giudicare i testi tradotti.

I vari canoni ed i testi stessi cambiano in rapporto dialettico continuo con i diversi criteri utilizzati. Non vi sono versioni finali e la valutazione di ogni traduzione deve tener conto del processo che l'ha originata e della sua funzione in un dato contesto.

I criteri di valutazione inoltre variano nel tempo; è infatti facilmente dimostrabile il fatto che sono stati utilizzati criteri diversi nelle diverse epoche.

La traduzione, pur avendo il suo nucleo nell'attività linguistica, appartiene piú propriamente alla semiotica, la scienza che studia i segni e le strutture, i processi e le funzioni dei segni (cf. Hawkes – *Structuralism and Semiotics*). Nello svolgere la sua attività il traduttore si serve quindi di criteri che trascendono quelli linguistici puri operando attraverso un processo di decodificazione e ricodificazione. Il modello che meglio schematizza questo procedimento è quello di Eugène Nida:

lingua di partenza- testo- analisi-transfer-ristrutturazione traduzione-lingua d'arrivo.

Vediamo ad esempio il caso del termine inglese 'hallo'. Il termine indica un saluto amichevole che si usa quando ci si incontra. I dizionari francesi riportano la traduzione 'ça va? ', quelli tedeschi "wie geht's, mentre in italiano abbiamo 'pronto/ ciao'. E' evidente che l'inglese non distingue tra quando ci si incontra faccia a faccia e quando si comunica attraverso il telefono; diversamente in italiano il termine 'pronto?' puó essere usato solo nel caso di una conversazione telefonica.

Il processo traduttivo si compone di diversi elementi:

1) la nozione, che in Ludskanov diventa trasformazione semiotica e in Jacobson trasposizione interlingue- dove si cerca l'invariante informativo
2) la funzione stilistica (comicità, appropriatezza) e il contesto sociale (comunicazione diretta o mediata ad es) faccia a faccia o telefono)
3) la classe sociale e gerarchica dei parlanti e il risultante 'peso' di un saluto a diversi livelli di società.

Sono queste, componenti assolutamente non trascurabili del processo di traduzione. Citando Saussure, la parola non puó essere semplicisticamente definita immagine + suono, ma va caratterizzata attraverso i rapporti sintagmatici (orizzontali), rapporti che ogni singolo termine stabilisce con le parole che lo circondano all'interno della frase e i rapporti associativi (verticali) che vengono definiti all'interno della struttura della lingua.

Vi sono poi i tratti associativi secondari. Prendiamo ad esempio il vocabolo inglese 'butter'. Nella cultura inglese 'butter' non indica semplicemente un prodotto commestibile , ma evoca i concetti di purezza, salute, alto valore di status (soprattutto se confrontato con la margarina). Traducendo il termine 'butter' con 'burro' indichiamo certamente un prodotto riconoscibile come tale anche in Italia e cioè un grasso cremoso commestibile, ma il contesto culturale cambia. In Italia il burro non è considerato un alimento 'nobile', non è salato, è giallognolo, quasi bianco e viene comunemente usato per cucinare; in Inghilterra invece è spesso di un giallo deciso, salato, si spalma sul pane e si usa raramente in cucina. Evidente, in questo caso la distinzione tra la funzione e il valore del prodotto nei due diversi contesti culturali esaminati.

La traduzione butter/burro è perfettamente valida ad un primo livello di traduzione, ma l'esempio ci dimostra che, come affermava Sapir, ogni lingua rappresenta una realtà diversa. Di questo dobbiamo tener conto non dimenticando poi la definizione di significato del famoso linguista inglese Firth secondo cui esso rappresenta un complesso di rapporti di vario genere tra i termini componenti un contesto di situazioni.

Il processo di traduzione centra costantemente la sua attenzione sul lettore o l'uditore è ció esige naturalmente che vi sia, tra il testo tradotto e il testo d'origine, esatta corrispondenza. La distinzione formulata da Catford tra traduzione letterale e traduzione libera è ben conosciuta da tutti, anche dai non addetti ai lavori, ma essa non prende in considerazione l'aspetto di trasformazione semiotica, che è una componente ormai riconosciuta nella traduzione. Popovic, nella sua definizione di equivalenza traduttiva, distingue quattro componenti:

1) Equivalenza linguistica, dove c'è omogeneità a livello linguistico sia nel testo di partenza che nel testo d'arrivo. E' questa la traduzione parola per parola.
2) Equivalenza paradigmatica, dove c'è equivalenza "negli elementi di un asse espressivo" cioè negli elementi grammaticali che Popovic valuta come categoria superiore all'equivalenza lessicale.
3) Equivalenza stilistica (traduttiva) dove c'è "equivalenza funzionale di elementi sia nell'originale che nella traduzione la quale mira ad un'identità espressiva con un'invariante di significato identico".
4) Equivalenza testuale (sintagmatica) dove c'è equivalenza nella strutturazione sintagmatica del testo e cioè equivalenza di forma e modello.

Neuburt cerca di risolvere il problema della equivalenza nelle traduzioni considerandola come una categoria semiotica, comprendendo le componenti sintattica, semantica, e pragmatica (secondo le categorie di Pierce) in un ordine gerarchico dove la componente semantica precede quella sintattica e quella pragmatica modifica le altre due.

La teoria della traduzione cerca di offrire al traduttore le condizioni per operare in modo ottimale, ma non ne risolve sostanzialmente i problemi poichè la traduzione è un lavoro pragmatico. Seguendo ancora la strada tracciata dalla Basnètt McGuire, cito Octavio Paz:

Ogni traduzione è quasi un'invenzione e come tale essa costituisce un testo unico.

Considerando il lato pratico dell'argomento, si puó affermare che il traduttore svolge il suo lavoro entrando in contatto con quasi tutti i settori della vita industriale, commerciale e professionale. Il suo settore tradizionale, quello letterario, che comprende testi umanistici, religiosi, romanzi, poesia, teatro, cinema e televisione, quantunque sia consistente ed in aumento, è attualmente sopraffatto dal volume e dall'importanza che la traduzione ha assunto in altri settori. Nel commercio, che in Italia significa esportazione, l'operatore deve essere a conoscenza, specialmente nell'ambito della CE, dell'inglese e del francese per essere in grado di stabilire contatti telefonici e via fax con l'estero e saper comprendere ed interpretare la documentazione transnazionale.

La documentazione puó essere il punto di partenza per chi deciderà di occuparsi in futuro del settore commerciale o di settori affini quali quelli bancario o assicurativo. E nella CE abbiamo documenti nei settori dei trasporti, delle assicurazioni, dei finanziamenti e della dogana che richiedono una conoscenza dell'inglese specialistico del settore interessato, vis-a-vis i termini usati nei contratti internazionali e transnazionali fra compratore e venditore.

I contratti coprono le condizioni non solo di vendita, ma anche di consegna, di responsabilità, di nolo, di divisione dei costi e le limitazioni contrattuali sia per il venditore che per il compratore. Questi contratti sono regolati da condizioni imposte attraverso accordi ben precisi chiamati INCOTERMS (International Commercial Terms) che facilitano gli scambi nel mondo occidentale. In tema di contratti, bisogna osservare che molti sono estremamente complessi e data la loro natura specifica non rientrano nella tipologia citata: è in questo caso che deve intervenire il traduttore.

Continuando l'elenco dei settori nei quali il traduttore opera quotidianamente, citiamo i bilanci delle società, delle banche, delle multinazionali (bilanci tradotti sempre in inglese), i preventivi industriali inviati all'estero, le descrizioni di macchinari ed attrezzature, i manuali di istruzioni all'uso, i certificati di garanzia e di qualità del prodotto, testi di responsabilità civile ecc...

In generale si puó affermere che tutti i campi di specializzazione in crescente sviluppo richiedono l'opera del traduttore. In medicina, chimica, farmacologia, agraria, biologia, molti lavori scientifici vengono tradotti con frequenza sempre maggiore ed inviati a colleghi e ad enti esteri o a riviste scientifiche e professionali, quali ad esempio la rivista medica inglese *Lancet*, per la pubblicazione. Nei settori medico e chirurgico, ad esempio, molte sono le traduzioni che descrivono nuove tecniche di intervento, sperimentazioni di nuovi farmaci o l'impiego di nuove attrezzature.

Questo discorso puó ovviamente essere esteso ad altri settori quali l'architettura, la moda, l'estetica ecc... Alcune riviste italiane di prestigio vengono già pubblicate in edizione inglese o, come nel caso della rivista ABITARE, in edizione multilingue, con traduzione testo a fronte in inglese e francese e con riassunti in spagnolo e tedesco.

La figura del traduttore dunque è oggi indispensabile. La sua importanza è in continua crescita e ci non stupisce se si pensa allo sviluppo crescente della comunità europea e del mercato comune le cui due lingue ufficiali, inglese e francese, rappresentano, insieme con lo spagnolo, le lingue più diffuse nel mondo.

Violence in the Art of Iris Murdoch

INTRODUCTION

In Stephen Heath's description (in *Le Nouveau Roman*), the novel constitutes a process with different or changing models of personality, causality and significance, that is, basically, a model of intelligibility[1]. "The primary semiotic agent of intelligibility is the novel". It is a semiotic process for philosophical and linguistic meaning, and for the production of a human world of signficance. "Le roman est la manière dont cette société se parle"[2]; and in Husserl's concept, coherence and significance is the "reactivation"[3] of models of intelligibility.

In general structuralist theory, a novel constitutes a hierarchy of systems containing domains or sub-systems of cultural models, including plot, theme and character. Structuralism has dealt with modernist writing which "turned its back on the traditional idea of art as imitation and substituted the idea of art as an autonomous activity"[4]; whereas traditionalism maintained that art must tell the truth about life (a classical tenet) and culminated in the great 19th century realist novel[5]. Iris Murdoch's work is part of anti-modernist writing, "advanced contemporary realistic mode"[6] as Professor Elizabeth Dipple defines her work, where the writer is the creator of reality[7].

Iris Murdoch uses the logical methods of causality, creates *Gestalts* for her personages and the action i.e. psychological

1. J.Culler, "The Poetics of the Novel" in *Structuralist Poetics*, Routledge Kegan Paul, London 1975.

2. S.Heath, *Le Nouveau Roman*, in J.Culler, *op. cit.* pp. 187-188.

3. Husserl, cited by J.Culler, *op. cit.* p. 190.

4. D.Lodge, *Working with Structuralism*, London, Routledge Kegan Paul, p. 5 f.

5. Sartre (in Culler, *op. cit.* p. 195) on the 19th century novel, "... it is told from the viewpoint of wisdom and experience and listened to from the viewpoint of order."

6. Elizabeth Dipple, *Iris Murdoch: Work for the Spirit*, Cape.

7. R.Young, *Untying the Text*, RKP p. 12, where Stephen Heath is quoted from *Vertige du Déplacement* p. 69 trans. R Young, "The removal of the human subject from the centre of the stage can{cont.}

schemata, her plots have a teleological determination, that is to say certain things happen in order that the *récit* may develop as it does. The significance of action in her novels may be described as functional in Propp's terms (when he explains the components of folk tales) i.e. a function is an act of *dramatis personae* defined by its significance for the course of action in the tale as a whole[8].

She is platonic in her attitude to art – it must have integrity i.e. be the imitation of life in the best sense. The core of her *opus* is dark, complex and wide-ranging. In her own words:

> I was a kind of existentialist and now I am a kind of platonist
> (interview with W.K.Rose in 1968)[9].

It is essentially the problem of good versus evil, in which evil is master of the world in its multifarious spirit-rending complexity, and is most often presented in widespread subtle forms of violence.

Her philosophical and theological readings are from St. John of the Cross, Julian of Norwich, Nietzsche and Heidegger, Sartre and Freud. Life is action; action is imperfect, tainted with evil, even unknowingly (unconscious forces discovered in the psyche by Freud), – an evil sublimated by Nietzsche into philosophy:

> Evil is energy, the best form of energy; ...man is bad, said the Sages.[10]

She refers allusively or indirectly in her novels to ideas from Heidegger, his *Dasein*, that is the existential choosing in a world without God (in which many of Iris Murdoch's "egomaniac Byronic" characters exist), trying to suppress the concept of death by living in the present energetically (*Sein*

{cont.} be said to have enabled what Stephen Heath has called the 'mythic site par excellence in our society' – the subject/author as originating consciousness, authority for meaning and truth,"

8. V.Propp, quoted by J.C.Culler *op. cit.* p. 208.

9. E.Dipple *op. cit.* p. 158, where Iris Murdoch is quoted in an interview with W.K.Rose in 1968.

10. F.Nietzsche, *Così parlò Zarathustra*, Italian edition of *Thus Spake Zarathustra*, Adelphi Edizioni, IV, parte 2.

und Zeit)[11]. Her treatment of violence is at times allusive and allegorical – the struggle of good and evil is often referred both in the treatment of the personages and the episodes to metaphysical planes. Her problem, to reach the goal of discernment is tackled by process, "to try, to invent, to work through our nature against our nature."[12] This seeming contradiction provokes the question, is Iris Murdoch covertly advocating a 'deconstructive' reading to the values contained in her work?

Iris Murdoch consciously follows the grand tradition (Shakespeare, the classics, the 19th century realist novel) with no little suggestion from the works of Sartre and Simone Weil [13].

Elizabeth Dipple says of Iris Murdoch's art:

> The ideological resting-place of her fiction is permanently fixed on an imageless good which she is prone to identify either with Plato or with the mystical *via negativa* of St. John of the Cross[14].

Iris Murdoch talks of "art...swept by the violence of divine grace"[15]. What constitutes violence in her novels, then? According to *The New Webster Dictionary of the English Language*, violence has the following variations of meaning:

> the quality of being violent, vehemence, intensity of action or motion, highly excited feeling, impetuosity, injury done to anything which is entitled to respect or reverence, profanation, violation,

11. Heidegger's *Sein und Zeit*, read by Pattie O'Driscoll in *The Time of the Angels*, in E.Dipple *op. cit.* pp. 62-3.

12. In I.Murdoch, *Nuns and Soldiers* (1980), where Christ is experienced mystically by Anne (an ex-nun) in episodes recalling the 'negative way' of Julian of Norwich and St. John of the Cross, and in the dark night of the soul of Brendan, a Catholic priest in *Henry and Cato* (1976).

13. Simone Weil cf. I.Murdoch *Against Dryness*, "Literature must always represent a battle between real people and images, and what it requires now is a much stronger and more complex conception of the former." *but* "L'imagination combleuse de vides est essentiellement menteuse. Elle exclut la troisième dimension car ce sont seulement les objects réels qui sont dans les trois dimsensions. Elle exclut les rapports multiples.", Simone Weil, *Cahiers*.

14. E.Dipple, *op. cit.* p. 47.

15. I.Murdoch, *The Fire and the Sun, Why Plato Banished the Artists*, 1977, p. 82.

unjust force, outrage, attack, assault[16].

I admit that Iris Murdoch uses many of these forms as components in the artistic structure of her novels.

MORAL/SPIRITUAL VIOLENCE

Iris Murdoch has written,

> One might say that true morality is a sort of unesoteric mysticism, having its source in an austere and unconsoled love of the Good[17].

Among the ethical or moral patterns of forces or values to be found in her work, truth/ deception, clarity/ ambiguity, honesty/ manipulation are structured as binary oppositions. These contrasting forces can be seen as a part of the code of communication, designating relationships in the text, exchange. Thus forces such as manipulation, untruthfulness and ambiguity are instruments of moral and spiritual violence not often detected at first because they are masked by the use of subtlety in performance. Many of Murdoch's characters believe in the Good. Rupert in *A Fairly Honourable Defeat* thinks it is attainable. Tallis, another 'good' character in the novel, is less sure. The platonic myth of the absolute, however, is inconceivable in the contemporary ethos, and its practicality in society today as a workable spiritual mediator is a scholastic illusion. Iris Murdoch states in *The Fire and the Sun* that the later Plato reaffirms his belief in objective values, which the wise can experience, but now after Plato, in non-classical epochs, Christians and liberal thinkers recognize the imperfection and limitations of the human spirit. For Plato "Wisdom is *there*, but belongs to gods and very few mortals" (Timaeus, *Laws*)[18]

The unattainability of the absolute, the relativity of human values, is at the root of the modern social crisis, and society's dynamism becomes progressively more destructive and violent. Violence is the road even to the achievement of positive values, Murdoch affirms indirectly in the narrative of her novels. For

16. *The New Webster Dictionary*, Grolier, New York.

17. Anne in *The Sovereignty of Good* (1970), p. 92.

18. I. Murdoch, *op. cit.* p. 41.

her art has always been a representation of contact between the human spirit and the absolute. Art has a moral purpose:

> Art can rarely, but with authority, show how we learn from pain, swept by the violence of divine grace toward an unwilling wisdom, as described in the first chorus of the *Agammemnon* in words which somehow remind us of Plato...[19].

The personage who represents (the actant) the violence of change of identity, mystification of intent, ambiguity of motivation in *A Fairly Honourable Defeat* (the novel which is our referent) is Julius, the "bad artist"[20], who is placed in opposition to the 'good' Rupert, a person who illudes himself that moral worth can be objectivised (he is writing a book on platonic ethics), that the good can be an ideal in life, and thus can be lived subjectively. Julius goes out of his way to demolish this false concept, this ideal image of existence that Rupert has created for himself. The moral violence that ensues is enacted in the manipulation of events, the use of untruthfulness and ambiguity of role. Julius manipulates information contained in old love letters (which he finds in Rupert's desk) written by Rupert to his wife Hilda, and Morgan's love letters to himself (when both he and Morgan were professors in America); arranges a clandestine meeting anonymously between Rupert and Morgan in the Prince Regent Museum; has an ambiguous and insincere friendship with Rupert's wife, Hilda; blackmails Simon because of his relationship with Axel.

Julius's ambiguous and equivocal role extends to his identity too. His identity is opaque and mystifying,

> I could never manage to see how Julius felt[21],

says Hilda to Rupert at the beginning of the novel when they are commenting on Julius's return to London. His transformation from being "famous, ... distinguished... a mythological presence"[22], a mysterious intelligent professor in everybody's

19. *ibid* p. 82.

20. Cf. E.Dipple, *op. cit.* p. 41.

21. *A Fairly Honourable Defeat* (abbreviated AFHD henceforth), p. 13.

22. E.Dipple *op. cit.* p. 18.

esteem, to being "unmasked" as a subtle evil trickster to Hilda by Tallis (Morgan's estranged husband) and to the reader, is a part of the hermeneutic code of the novel. (Julius has the problem of getting rid of Morgan, his ex-lover, and in the process of socializing cannot resist showing superiority by belittling and destroying Rupert's book on ethics (and Rupert himself), in his avowed object of stirring up the complacent bourgeois world of the English upper middle class).

Axel (a civil servant like Rupert) is the only one who from the first sees the evil potentiality of Julius's genius and in his dialogue with his friend Simon (Rupert's young brother) foreshadows Julius's evil role:

> He would not be a man to have as an enemy... ruthless and cynical... Julius isn't a compromiser.[23]

Julius is an ex-refugee from a wartime Nazi concentration camp[24] who passes on his loss of moral sensibility to others, forcing events in this way. He likes power over others. It is interesting to note what Iris Murdoch has written in *The Unicorn,* in the words of Max Lejour who is defining courtly love's platonic meaning, and touches upon Até, a Greek divinity who torments humanity:

> Recall the idea of Até which was so real to the Greeks. Até is the name of the almost automatic transfer of suffering from one being to another. Power is a form of Até. The victims of power, and any power has victims, are themselves infected. They have to pass it on, to use power on others. This is evil...[25]

The process of moral degeneration is imposed on Rupert by Julius, partly by his sense of superiority and also by his machinations abetted unwittingly by Hilda and Morgan. It is interesting to note that in *The Fire and the Sun* Murdoch, after Plato (*The Republic, Theetetes*), defines evil as the way good

23. AFHD p. 34.

24. *ibid.* p. 430. Julius talking to Tallis, "I spent the war in Belsen".

25. I.Murdoch, *The Unicorn,* Penguin p. 97, cited by E.Dipple *op. cit.* pp. 114-6. *The Unicorn* concerns mainly a woman, Hannah, who is trying to escape from the guilt attached to her actions in the past and cannot. She commits suicide.

degenerates into egoism and cynicism leading to a state of confusion[26]. Rupert dies for his ideal of the good,

> I won't accept the second-rate[27]

and this attitude, or blindness to reality consumes the tragedy of the 'good' man defeated by evil. The actions of Julius in the novel, with their subtle ambiguous effects and far-reaching if unexpected tragic conclusion identifies him as a violator of the spirit, a destroyer of human souls.

Manifesting his arrogance and egoism, as well as his role of man-about-the-world who can be generous even to people he has offended, and showing the minimum compunction over the tragic results of his gratuitous interference in others' lives, Julius sees himself as justified (an ironic touch of Iris Murdoch's) in a dialogue with Tallis at the end of the novel:

> You concede that I am an instrument of justice?
> Tallis smiled[28].

In his progressive role of demonic evil-doer, Julius takes on an allegorical significance, he plays the part of Satan, the supreme genius of evil. Julius despises society, seeing it as decadent and near its historical end as an epoch, and even as civilization, and in the role of a dangerous 'joker', he radically destroys the lives of Rupert, Hilda, Morgan and Tallis, the "dwellers in the vaults of *eikasia*" (as pointed out by E.Dipple[29], they who live in the "cosy dreaming ego")[30].

Julius, a Iago-like character, seems to perceive his devilish role by the end of the novel, and the symbol of Satan seems to be intended by Iris Murdoch when he makes a prediction which breaks out of the limits of the novel:

> I suppose in the nature of things we shall meet again... ... I may take on another big assignment soon[31].

26. E.Dipple *op. cit.* p. 193 quotes I.Murdoch in *The Fire and the Sun.*

27. AFHD p. 382.

28. *ibid.* p. 431.

29. E.Dipple *op. cit.* p. 105.

30. I.Murdoch, *The Fire and the Sun*, pp. 79-80.

31. (following E.Dipple) AFHD p.431.

He seems to represent a force which exists outside fiction, a real evil power, engaged seriously in battling with the good forces. And Iris Murdoch will tackle the mystery of evil in another work of art.

In *A Fairly Honourable Defeat*, Morgan too acts with violence, especially towards Tallis, her husband. She leaves him for Julius and later uses him to support her vain confused egoistic ends, encouraged by the fact that Tallis is still friendly towards her and seems to forgive her wild behaviour[32]. However she has an obsessive guilt complex, because she feels unjustified in her bad treatment of Tallis. Her personality is unstable – she suffers and makes him suffer. In a conversation with Hilda (her sister) she tries to analyse her situation and her past life with him:

MORGAN	...But really, Tallis is ineffaceable .....
HILDA	Do you feel guilty about Tallis? You mustn't.
MORGAN	Why not? I am guilty. No, it's deeper than guilt, Hilda. His consciousness binds mine even now. It sounds like an obsession[33].

Morgan, an uncertain personality in herself, is a victim of moral and spiritual violence to herself, to Tallis and to others.

PHYSICAL VIOLENCE

Violence, murder, incest, injury (essential elements in classical literature, Shakespeare's histories and tragedies, and in the realist novel) are reported daily in modern life, and are an indispensable ingredient in Iris Murdoch's fiction. Physical violence is often employed as a component of the action in her novels, and numerous instances of suicide, murder and accidental death could be quoted. Of course these incidents are woven into the fabric of the meaning of the work and have their justification as part of the hermeneutic code.

In *A Fairly Honourable Defeat* Rupert commits suicide in his garden swimming pool, out of "vanity" says Julius, the

32. *ibid.* p. 14 cf. a dialogue between Rupert and Hilda,

R. Tallis would forgive her.
H. Oh forgiveness... What's the use of that?

33. *ibid.* p. 58.

machinator of events which provoke it. The reader has doubts that this is true. Rupert does indeed seem to have lost all he loved and lived for, his wife Hilda, his ideal of the 'good' to be embodied in a book which is a failure, his comfortable way of life. The crisis of identity is provoked gratuitously by Julius. The cruelty of Rupert's fate seems to prove that Iris Murdoch is stating indirectly that life will not support platonic illusions. Rupert's 'philosophy', the belief that the 'good' in life exists and that we can experience it as an ideal, is destroyed[34].

In another episode, Simon, (Rupert's young brother and Axel's boyfriend) offended by Julius' domineering, insidious and treacherous friendship (he tries to separate him from Axel) is provoked to uncharacteristic violence[35]. He takes his revenge for being blackmailed and harassed by Julius, by pushing him into Rupert's swimming pool at a garden party one afternoon.

More significantly, Tallis who abhors violence of any nature (his mind has been seared by his sister's rape and murder in her adolescence), intervenes with contained violence[36] to stop the escalation of physical conflict in a Chinese restaurant to defend the 'good', a coloured Jamaican who is being attacked by some white youths.

It is notable that in the same novel, physical violence is often an escalation of action in defence of what is believed to be 'good', to obtain 'good' results, or in a 'good' cause. In another instance, Tallis reveals his human side when, despite good intentions and against his better nature, he gives vent to his latent resentment of Morgan's ambiguous behaviour to him and others and struggles with her to prevent her leaving his house after asking for and not getting an explanation for her treatment of him[37].

Physical violence takes the form of hysteria, and there are many examples of tears, rages, furniture breaking and similar

34. D.Lodge, *op. cit.* p. 57 cites Lévi-Strauss, "(who) has pointed out that myths are 'our way of accepting contradictions between experience and belief'".

35. AFHD p. 373.

36. *ibid.* p. 241.

37. *ibid.* p. 285.

incidents which express the drama of confused emotions for Morgan and Hilda, and Simon and Axel. The incompatibility between Morgan and Tallis takes on self-violent images of death, physical suffocation, removal of presence, and masochistic suffering when both Morgan and Tallis, in their heart-to-heart talk analyse the breakdown of their marriage.

Morgan says to Tallis:

> When I married you I felt I was killing myself. It seemed somehow wonderful at the time. But I couldn't kill myself. I have to be........free, free, free[38].

Whatever the specific act of physical violence, whatever its horrific effect on the reader (surprise/ suspense/ disgust/ rejection) the violence is not uncalled for in the author's intentions, but serves a precise artistic purpose, a turning point in the narrative or in the identity or role of a personage – there is a teleological determination. The violence often informs the crises and is a necessary component of the tragic human world presented in Iris Murdoch's fiction.

RHETORICAL VIOLENCE

There is a suspicion of rhetorical violence, a 'deconstruction' effect in the art of Iris Murdoch. The impression of ambiguity in the structure and meaning of the novels, is partly due to Murdoch's modification of platonic ideas, i.e. Plato makes the ideal of the Good the supreme value of human existence, whereas she goes one step further by offering a Nietzschean slant on the effect that art as statement in language can have,

> ... the greatness of great art may be an ephemeral illusion[39],

namely, that all language presents appearances, is a part of the mental process of the author and the reader. Nietzsche's insight that language is ambiguous could be pertinent to the understanding of Murdoch's theory of writing.

38. *ibid.* p. 214.

39. I.Murdoch, *The Sovereignty of Good*, pp. 72-3.

Nietzsche in *The Will to Power*[40] affirms that statements can be both performative and constative at the same time (cf. Austin[41]), so undermining the objective of truth value of language and consequently of works of art, as constructs or signification, i.e. the reality presented as wholly subjective. (cf. the willing suspension of disbelief of Coleridge so necessary in romantic literature).

In Iris Murdoch's novels, the action, the hermeneutic code has its effect on the reader, i.e. the resolutions (peripeteia) are puzzling or even ambiguous, undecidable, or lead to reflection on changes of identity or on the partial resolutions of conflicts at spiritual levels, leaving the reader to hypothesize that the novel (in this case *A Fairly Honourable Defeat*) is tending to be (unbeknownst to itself maybe!) a single imprecise trope, provoking doubt. *A Fairly Honourable Defeat* seen has haphazardly structured on different literal and figural levels, leaves a feeling of 'deconstructive' uneasiness; its interpretation at solely realistic level is not satisfactory either to the writer (seemingly) or the reader. This 'breakdown' of the art form is evidenced by the fact that solutions offered to problems awaken dissatisfaction in the reader, reflecting confusion or doubt at authorial level, creating a feeling of aporia all round, i.e. is non-resolution a readerly/ writerly ending? – can non-resolution be an image for doubt?

In *A Fairly Honourable Defeat* there is an unemphasised use of allegory (the opposition of good/ evil, as played out by the trinity Tallis (Christ), Julius (Satan) and Morgan (the human soul)). Tallis, a simple self-sacrificing man lives his life humbly and poorly, and thus is more convincing as a symbol, to the extent that he seems to be 'de-mythologised' through his credibility, in contrast to the opaqueness of the devil symbol Julius, and the self-centredness of the lost soul Morgan. Naturally as a 'personage' he is less interesting and less attractive to the reader (in fact his living in squalor repels us, and his obtuse suffering suffocates Morgan; Julius despises and

40. Nietzsche, in *The Will to Power* (Fragments 516 and 477) cited by Paul de Man in *Action and Identity in Nietzsche*, in R.Young, *op. cit.* p. 267.

41. Austin cited by P.de Man In R.Young, *op. cit.* . p. 267.

later patronises him). In contrast both Morgan and Julius are more dynamic, the latter assuming aspects of a 'brilliant Miltonic archangel of darkness'.

> Tallis has no myth[42]

says Morgan, underscoring the spiritual preoccupations of the novel.

The moral or ethical theme ends in tragedy. Rupert who is a platonic humanist, who believes in the final triumph of platonist ideals is defeated. The bourgeois values of the novel are destroyed in this way.

The valorisation of the novel becomes complex because personages act with ambiguous effects, cf. the untruthfulness of Morgan – who deceives herself to the extent that she has serious psychological problems of identity (she identifies with Tallis and marries him, then after alienation, with Julius who she persecutes; later with the 'good' in Rupert; finally she attaches herself to Hilda to return and evoke their childhood happiness together). In a sense the novel does not solve her problems, except in so far as she finds a dubious (to the reader) "freedom", returning to a relationship consolidated in childhood. Her function in the novel presents the enigma of identity in her search for self-realisation. The ambiguity of identity is played out at different levels by other characters too – Julius, dissatisfied by society wanders from nation to nation. He cannot socialise happily and finally prefers to be alone,

> He was happy for the present, to be by himself in Paris... life was good[43].

When he moves in society, he acts with deleterious effects, disseminating evil (there is an implicit apology for this, when Julius recalls his past to Tallis, when Tallis sees the number tattooed on his arm during his imprisonment in a Nazi concentration camp) which is borne out by his manipulation of Rupert and Simon. The fairly obvious allegory, the triumph of evil, reveals a 'deconstructive' use of the idea of a moribund Trinity, implying that Christianity has little place among modern

42. AFHD cited by Dipple, *op. cit.* p. 18.

43. AFHD p. 447.

values. The presentation and description of the identity of Morgan as through Tallis's eyes as a person who is a misinterpreter of reality, who is a paradox, also seems to have a 'deconstructive' aspect. Morgan is by profession a philologist who cannot handle words with precision, cannot analyse herself. Tallis is perspicacious in this regard:

> There's something absolutely wrong here... you don't understand the meaning of the words you use... I think you are mistaken about your nature. You need deep belongingness and correction and stability... I think you're hopelessly theory-ridden[44].

However Morgan cannot reach self-knowledge – there is doubt she will ever do so at the end of the novel, when she rejoins Hilda. She seems to be over-emphatic when she writes decisively to her sister, "Darling, hang on. We will not be divided[45]."

Certainly re-readings seems to be necessary to pinpoint what Murdoch intends. And this leads to important questions. Is deconstructive criticism possible/ pertinent to her work? Is she de-mystifying bourgeois values in *A Fairly Honourable Defeat*? Or is there only a pandemic circulation of signs in her art?

VIOLENCE AS PROCESS

In *A Fairly Honourable Defeat*, the use of classical myth and Shakespearean archetypes (cf. the parallel between Iago/ Julius – both evil instigators – and Othello/ Rupert – both die through evil machination –) has pertinency and cogency. At the conclusion of the novel, violence not love is triumphant, with the exception of the Axel/ Simon relationship which is underlined by the classical parallel of the Apollo/ Marsyas myth [46].

Axel insists on honesty in their love, and this 'truth' saves them, this purging of illusion in their relationship brings them to a better understanding and happiness, although Simon, younger and unstable, suffers, to win through. Following Elizabeth

44. *ibid.* p. 213.

45. *ibid.* p. 389.

46. E.Dipple *op. cit.* p. 108.

Dipple, here is the passage[47] in which Simon playfully evokes the myth:

> You're Apollo and I'm Marsyas. You'll end by flaying me.
>
> That's an image of love, actually, Apollo and Marsyas.
>
> How do you mean?
>
> The agony of Marsyas is the inevitable agony of the human soul in its desire to achieve God.
>
> The things you know.
>
> The things you failed to learn at the Courtauld.
>
> I don't believe it though. Someone is flayed really. And there's only blood and pain and no love.
>
> You think our planet is like that.
>
> I think our planet is like that.
>
> No redeeming grace?
>
> None at all.
>
> None, Simon?
>
> Well, only this kind.

This is a strong almost direct statement from Iris Murdoch, that only suffering will bring love on a human level, and only suffering will bring union with Good/ God on a metaphysical level.

The subtle evil, embodied in Julius' actions and their effects is brought about by his interference in others' lives. His machinations change radically or destroy the lives of Rupert, Hilda and Morgan (Tallis however resists him and holds on to his integrity if weakly). Julius's actions could be seen as part of the hermeneutic code in the novel – the process of solving enigmas, finding solutions to problems and crises, to bring about the peripeteia (cf. Propp's analysis of the hermeneutic process – *le dévoilement* – where narrator, character or reader accepts a satisfactory solution[48]).

Turning to another novel, in *The Black Prince*[49], the pro-

47. AFHD p. 41.

48. J.Culler, *op. cit.* p. 208.

49. I.Murdoch, *The Black Prince.* The novel is one of 'persecution'. The personages nurse manifest and violent antipathies for one another was well as friendship. Bradley Pearson, morose and anti-{continued}

tagonist refers to the Apollo/ Marsyas myth too. Bradley Pearson pays with suffering for his lifelong ambition to write a good, serious book, his great work of art which turns out to be the novel *The Black Prince* itself – a realist tale, with modernist deconstructive aspects – intrusions by the narrator using different narrating voices, the invention of personae who are Bradley Pearson himself and who reflect different aspects of his or the author's viewpoint. The novel in this way expresses Murdoch's wish to emphasise the ambiguity of multifaceted life, its appearance and reality. Through Loxias Iris Murdoch addresses the reader directly to explain why a novel is written,

> Man's creative sturggle, his search for wisdom and truth, is a love story.[50]

The process of identity change, the path of the plot in *The Black Prince* is fraught with violent episodes. Violence is part of a process which transforms horrifically and tragically the lives of all the characters; death dominates the conclusions of the novel (Bradley Pearson, old and very ill, dies in prison), but there is a triumph of art, the aim of Murdoch and Pearson 'the author', for the book is written. Art, the only genuine creative activity spurred on by love wins by becoming manifest. The novel is Iris Murdoch's book on her theory of art, which, she says, is the only fixed point of significance in the modern world where all other values – Christian, philosophical, ethical, moral, social are dying or dead or false.

CONCLUSION

The novel is a semiotic process to produce meaning in the human world, through art, it meets the reader's expectation of a world; to produce a model of the social world, and models of personages. Plot, theme, character and their functions may be

{cont.} social destroys Arnold Baffin's novels (a rival successful author and friend). Arnold is murdered by Rachel, his wife, out of unrequited love, later hate for Bradley, who seduces Julian, Arnold's and Rachel's 20 year old daughter, who is less than half his age. Bradley is tried and imprisoned for Arnold's murder.

50. *The Black Prince*, p. 9. Loxias is the name of B.Pearson's editor. Loxias met Pearson in prison and publishes the book after Pearson's death.

studied by detecting the existence of codes for interpretation and structuration, as described by Barthes[51]. In order to group together items of a single kind in the interests of homogeneity and reading, Barthes has identified five main 'codes' applied to the reading of the text. Each code is a general semantic structure allowing the reader to pick out items existing in the functional space which the code maps out. (In fact, Barthes added other codes or sub-codes to the text analysis).

1. the proairetic code – this corresponds to the reader's construction of the plot.
2. the hermeneutic code – this traces the logic of question and answer, enigma and solution, suspense and peripeteia, and is pertinent to the structure of the plot.
3. the semic code – in which models of semic features relating to persons, or developing characters can be applied to the personages in the novels.
4. the symbolic code – which in the areas of character and theme extrapolates symbolic and thematic readings of the text.
5. the referential code which gives coherence and significance to the cultural background the text refers to (often a collective cultural voice).

The terms distinguished can be divided (following Benveniste) into distributional (related to other items before or later in the text) and intregrative (taken up and grouped with analogous items in paradigms)[52].

Perhaps one could see Iris Murdoch's novels as basically contructed on a binary opposition (the four-term homology of Greimas[53] could illustrate this). She is fundamentally concerned at different levels with Life/ Death and Non-life (struggle for freedom)/ non-death (failure in life). This, to point out that more resonance should be given to her purpose in writing, her artistic objectives, the "high seriousness" of her themes, i.e. God and the Devil, Good versus Evil, the Nature of Love; to reveal her profound interest and capacity in presenting the

51. Barthes in J.Culler, *op. cit.* p. 203.

52. Benveniste in *ibid.*

53. Greimas cited by D.Lodge in *op. cit.* p. 18.

psychological level in action and in depicting the transformation of identity, the unconscious, i.e. the Freudian basis of her art, and the importance of her novels as sociological documents of middle-class contemporary English society; her value in continuing the 'grand' tradition. All this provokes a number of questions for the critic. Is her structural strategy covertly aiming at the de-mythologisation of the realistic text? After all she does not present 'normality' in her human world: 'energy' or violence seems often to move and motivate her personages (to the disgust of many readers!).

And, why apply structural methodology for analysing Iris Murdoch's novels? Can we see a writerly text, i.e. "the free play of signifiers and of *différance*" in her texts? In a dialogue between the two narrative voices of Bradley Pearson[54], she seems to reveal her own thoughts on the function and essence of art:

> Art.. is the telling of truth, and is the only available method for the telling of certain truths[55].

The Black Prince is, under certain aspects, Murdoch's fictional manifesto and supports the seriousness of purpose with which contemporary novel-writing as literature is invested by her. She defines the function of positive critcism through Loxias' contempt for "self-serving postscript writers" who reduce the importance of good writing[56].

Finally, can we section her text into lexias and codes *à la Barthes* for reading purposes? Can we pluralise the reader's intakes? and does Iris Murdoch (un)consciously tend to fragmentation in the structure (i.e. narrative, identity, theme, "*significance*") of her novels, creating images of doubt – *aporia*?

54. *The Black Prince*, p. 55.

55. E.Dipple *op. cit.* p. 115-6.

56. Compare *The Fire and the Sun* p. 78 where Murdoch maintains that art is superior to philosophy in the search for truth, "the calm, open judging mind of the intelligent experienced critic, united, as far as possible by theory" is "the final best instrument" of criticism.

SYNOPSIS (of the novels referred to in this article).

The novel *A Fairly Honourable Defeat* (1970) is the story of Julius, a brilliant professor, whose busy role disturbs the complacency of upper middle-class London, represented by the solid marriage of Rupert and Hilda, which is marred only by Peter, their son, who lives in his friend's house (Tallis), rather than continue his studies at Cambridge, and by Morgan, Hilda's sister and Julius's ex-lover. Morgan is married to Tallis, a social worker and teacher, who lives in squalor, and who tries to win back her affections, but she prefers to go and live with Hilda after Rupert's suicide. It is Julius's actions that constitute the interest of the plot, and indirectly provoke Rupert's death and shake up the lives of the other personaages, including Axel and Simon whose close relationship is reinforced with renewed faith in each other.

The Unicorn (1963) is a novel about guilt and murder, and expiation (embodied by a vague confused platonic worship of beauty and the good in life) which ends tragically. The protagonist, Hannah Crean-Smith, lives in a desolate part of the country and surrounds herself with friends and servants hoping to transform her unfortunate marriage and violent past into sublimated suffering. Despite her efforts (for she is bored not tormented), and those of Marian, her newly-arrived companion, and of others, friends, such as Effingham Cooper and servants and local people such as Gerald Scottow, the Lejour family and her relatives Violet and Jamesie, the dark evil forces, symbolised partly by her violent husband, Peter Crean-Smith, and her own confused self, and partly by the hostile nature of the countryside, create an apocalyptic climax to this story, one of Murdoch's most Freudian, which ends in the murder of her husband (who returns after a long absence) by her friend Nolan (who hopes to spare her suffering) and her murder of the domineering Gerald Scottow (who has become her gaoler) and her own desperate suicide.

The Black Prince, written in 1973, reveals Murdoch's modernistic approach (Freudian psychology, more prominence given to the Narrator, more importance to the Reader). It deals with the complications of love/ hate relationships in life and art (writing). The hero and narrator is a failed writer, Bradley Pearson, an elderly eccentric now living alone who wishes, undisturbed, to write his "great book". His friends (and his ex-wife) make this difficult. Wishing to "get away", (he elopes with 20 year-old Julian, Arnold and Rachel's daughter), he is imprisoned after being unjustly condemned for the murder of his friend, the writer Arnold Baffin (killed by his wife Rachel, whose love for Bradley is unreciprocated). In prison Bradley meets Loxias who publishes his "great book" (which is in fact *The Black Prince* we are reading) after Bradley's death.

Henry and Cato (1976) is about love, a salvation or a demonic force? Henry and Cato, childhood friends, meet up years later when Henry, now an 'art historian', in the USA returns to inherit family wealth and Stephanie, his dead brother's mistress. Cato, now a Catholic priest, believes in the salvation of love, in the form, however, of 'beautiful Joe', whose heart is not as angelic as his face. Cato is fatally disillusioned by both his religious faith and his love for Joe, who commits suicide. Henry, after an interlude with Stephanie, finally marries kind and courageous Colette, Cato's young sister.

Nuns and Soldiers (1980) The thesis in this novel is that happiness is not permanent but can be found at various stages and levels of life, and that it depends on individual decisions, of a spiritual and personal nature. Anne is an ex-nun who loses contact with God. Gertrude has tragically lost her husband. Both want to help others by good works. The 'Count' is a Polish exile who loves Gertrude silently, but she falls in love with Tim, a failed artist, who hopes to live off his rich friends with his mistress, Daisy. Tim and Gertrude finally marry, but Anne, though in love with the 'Count' prefers lonely independence.

BIBLIOGRAPHY

Novels by Iris Murdoch – Penguin Editions, London.
A Severed Head (1961)
The Unicorn (1963)
The Time of the Angels (1966)
A Fairly Honourable Defeat (1970)
The Sovereignty of Good (1970)
The Black Prince (1973)
Henry and Cato (1976)
Nuns and Soldiers (1980)

Other works by Iris Murdoch to which reference has been made.
The Fire and the Sun: Why Plato banished the Artists, 1977.
"Against Dryness: A Polemical Sketch," *Encounter*, 16 Jan. 1961, 16-20.

Belsey, C., *Critical Practice*, Methuen.
Culler, J., *Structuralist Poetics*, Routledge Kegan Paul 1975.
Dipple, E., *Iris Murdoch, Work for the Spirit*, Methuen 1982.
Hawkes, T., *Structuralism in Semiotics*, Methuen 1977.
Hoey, M., "Three Metaphors for Examining the Semantic Organization of Monologue", *Analysis 1* 1983, ETS Pisa.
Johnson, A., "Broken Images. Discursive Fragmentation and Paradigmatic Integrity in the Poetry of T.S.Eliot" in *Letteratura e Seduzione & Disourse Analysis*, Atti, VI Congresso Nazionale, AIA 1983.
"W.B.Yeats's 'The Magi'" in *Analysis 3* 1985.
Leech, G. *Semantics*, Penguin 1974.
Lodge, D., *Working with Structuralism*, Routledge Kegan Paul 1981.
Manferlotti, S., "The Victory of the Minotaur; George Orwell's *1984*" in *Analysis 1* 1984.
Maronni, F. "Henry James e le Possibilità dell'Inganno – Una lettura di *The Aspern Papers*" in *Analysis 3, 1985.*
Murdoch, I., *Il Fuoco e il Sole*, Sugar, Milano (Ital. trans. of *The Fire and the Sun*, OUP 1977).
Nietzsche, F., *Così parlò Zarathustra*, Adelphi 1985.
Weil, S., *Cahiers*, Paris.
Young, R. *Untying the Text*, Routledge Kegan Paul 1981.

Little Dorrit and Victorian England*

Up to the 1950s, the Victorian Age was regarded as a phase of the past which had been negative in that it had produced the most serious political and social problems of the 20th century. The Victorians saw themselves positively however, as the creators of a new and better world. They created the new middle class, the liberals, whose commercial ideals would transform the world. The Victorians had renewed faith in the achievements of mankind, in science, trade and progress, and in men in particular. England in the famous phrase was the "workshop of the world", leading nations to a modern utopia based on industry and material improvement. However, the moral and spiritual question was not ignored, and Matthew Arnold, with Thomas Carlyle, William Morris, Disraeli and others, later criticised the philistinism of the brash new English society, seen by Arnold as "drugged with business". Dickens relentlessly stormed against and satirised this amoral philistine society in his novels and writings, where he described and parodied an England of self-righteousness and unfeelingness, which was at the basis of Victorian complacency.

Where did this complacency spring from? Its philosophical basis is to be found in the contemporary philosophical climate of utilitarianism or Benthamism, after Jeremy Bentham[1] who maintained that all legislation should try to promote "the greatest happiness of the greatest number". In the economic sphere, the "laissez-faire" doctrine of Adam Smith *et alia* was at the basis of commercial liberalism. This progressive view of free trade was supported by economists such as Richard Cobden[2]:

* Lecture given on 25th Oct. 1985 at Salzburg University, Austria.

1. *Jeremy Bentham* – English philosopher and economist (1784-1832) dedicated to reform of law and government on Utilitarian principles. His great work was *Introduction to the Principles of Moral and Legislation*, 1789 in which he stated that human nature was governed by two masters, Pain and Pleasure, and that legislation must foresee that human action will tend to favour pleasure, and therefore ought to be based on practical rules. Utilitarianism postulated "the greatest happiness for the greatest number of people".

2. *Richard Cobden* – English economist and politician (1804-1865) a supporter of Free Trade and the abolition of customs duties; anti-corn-law lobbyist; supported Italian independence.

> Commerce is the grand panacea which, like a beneficent medical discovery will serve to inoculate with the healthy and saving taste for civilization all the nations of the world.

The expansion of commerce was in large measure achieved by the late 19th and early 20th century Western society, and the power of steam, coal and iron and steel radically transformed the modern world, the increase of trade being unprecedented. The price paid was the creation of large industrial masses who lived for work, and became the armies of the poor in times of economic crisis. Another important aspect of Victorian life was religion. Liberalism was reflected in this sphere too. Disraeli[3] introduced the Catholic Emancipation Bill, and it became a popular issue together with the interest in the independence of countries in Europe seeking political autonomy, especially Italy. Dickens took a genuine and often active notice of these contemporary mid-Victorian issues, which included education and poor relief. In England, the religious scene was varied; there were various protestant churches and chapels, High or Anglo-Catholic, low or dissenting churches, among which were the new dissenters, Methodists whose members were the working classes. '"Secular religion", as Hegel[4] called modern religion, was seen as personal virtue, personal salvation, which set a high value on religious probity, which was at the base of the Victorian cult of respectability.

These contemporary issues form a substantial part of the subject matter of Dickens' novel *Little Dorrit*, in which mid-Victorian London society is satirised and parodied.

Little Dorrit, Dickens' 11th novel, is based on Dickens' long experience of life in London, on his interest in parliamentary debate, his feeling for the fate of the poor, his sympathy for the middle-class Victorian ideals of love and family life. The novel was first published in serial form

3. *Benjamin Disraeli* – politician and writer (1804-1881) of Venetian origin; founder of "Young England" Conservative party, Conservative Prime Minister and friend of Queen Victoria; wrote an autobiographical caricature *Endymion* at the end of his life.

4. *Georg Hegel* – German philosopher (1770-1831) – immanentism and idealism characterise his philosophy. "Whatever is rational is real, what is real is rational"; "Truth is self-awareness".

between December 1855 and June 1857 and despite much criticism, it remains one of Dickens' most ambitious and successful novels. Part of its success today may rest on the fact that it is a sociological view of England, London in particular, of some importance and that the subject matter of the novel is based on real-life happenings and real places. In time the novel is placed in the 1820s but the political events portrayed reflect scandals in the financial world of the 1840s and 50s. The London Marshalsea Debtor's prison scenes are based on Dickens' young memories of that place, where his father had been imprisoned for debt. In his novel, *Little Dorrit*, the 20 year-old heroine is born in the Marshalsea, where entire families of debtors lived for years, because they could not pay their debts. Little Dorrit herself had known no other home, and remained there until her family is helped to an inheritance by the friendly interest of Arthur Clennam who later falls in love with her. The human theme of love and marriage is found less interesting today and goes under the name of sentimentalism or worse, sentimentality which critics have said Dickens indulged in too much. It is Dickens' creative reply to the heartlessness and brutality of the new industrial age. Not everybody was making a profit from the new iron foundries, the railways and overseas trade. The agricultural classes were being forced to leave the land and become the new proletariat of the rapidly expanding industrial cities all over England, forming the new displaced poor who worked from dawn to dusk for subsistence wages – a fact noted by Karl Marx[5] in London in the 40s onwards, and documented in detail in his writings. Against this background of degraded social and urban life in London Dickens comments on the unhappiness of social and family relationships by developing the theme of personal unhappiness (epitomised by Arthur's tragic relationship with his presumed mother, Mrs. Clennam) and the choice an individual has at times to find salvation in personal contacts, which become the theme of Arthur's love for Little Dorrit, whose reciprocating love culminates in their marriage. The rarity of true love is

5. *Karl Marx* – politician and writer (1818-1883), wrote *Das Kapital*, a critique of political economy in which capitalism is seen as outdated and destined to fail as a politico economic force.

therefore interwoven with protest against the alienating quality of life in London, because of incompetence and corruption in government, finance and politics, and what we could today call lack of planning. Commerce and its resultant corrupting effect on traditional *mores* are under fire in Dickens' work.

The heroine of the novel is Little Dorrit. She has a symbolic and structural importance as she represents the novel's affirmation of positive values – moral and social values. She is vital. She helps people unselfishly; she is outgoing. She comforts her old father and helps her sister and brother (both less reciprocating than herself) by going out of prison and working. This is how she meets Arthur, when she goes to work in Arthur's mother's Mrs Clennam's house. Later she helps Arthur along the steep road of personal recuperation from depression, hopelessness and moral weakness. It is salvation through personal participation – for Arthur too is a genuine and sincere person who helps people with true philanthropy – in contrast with false philanthropy represented in the novel by Casby, the Patriarch (a minor character in the novel of the typical exploiter of the poor – a person who owns slum property and makes money out of the rents). Little Dorrit is a creative being – she lives her virtues of goodness and self-sacrifice – her tenderness is genuine. She represents the idealised portrait of the good woman adored by the Victorians – in fact she is called the Little Mother of the Marshalsea. She is reminiscent of portraits of working-class women found in Mayhew's writings in *Characters of London's Labour and London's Poor*[6] – hard-working and self-sacrificing. Dickens sees her as an inspiration, something poetic and spiritual, almost possessed of divine angelic power – a symbol of the existence of higher values:

> It is enough that she was inspired to be something which was not what the rest were, and to be that something, different and laborious, for the sake of the rest. Inspired? Yes.[7]

6. *Henry Mayhew*, social historian and reporter, wrote *London Labour and the London Poor* (1851), and *London's Underworld* (1862).

7. *Charles Dickens: Little Dorrit*, Oxford 1982, p.59.

Dickens goes on to say inspiration is not only aesthetic or religious but can be that of human love for one's fellow creatures – the vocation of true brotherhood:

> Shall we speak of the inspiration of a poet or a priest, and not of the heart impelled by love and self-devotion to the lowliest work in the lowliest way of life![8]

Little Dorrit flowers in not only loving her family, but in loving and helping people around her. She brightens the gloom of life in prison with her helping hand and loving care, her good thoughts about others. As a personage, she is more difficult to appreciate, – she is a model of purity and unselfishness, she totally lacks egocentricity. Because she has this marked virtue of selflessness, not often observed and still less valued today, she tends to take on a symbolic quality for the literary critic, and contemporary taste sees Little Dorrit as representative of Victorian and traditional Christian ideals. The Dickensian model lacks the thrill and thrall of sex interest and a violent view of the world; Dickens' presentation of reality is thus old-fashioned, outdated and artistically uninteresting. Only too frequently modern literature stands off from moral discussion or ethical and religious or metaphysical interest. It prefers to use material such as that basically described in Dante's *Inferno*[9] rather than that found in his *Paradiso* so to say, – in any case violence has a shock or surprise effect lacking in the narration of moral action and virtue. Little Dorrit's individuality exists nevertheless and is portrayed on a psychological plane; she is an anima-like power, who inspires saving grace; she has that natural untrained religious quality admired by liberal intelligent Victorians (could we say that she is Dickens' Victorian version of Dante's Beatrice?). The virtuous woman was a Victorian ideal (perhaps a reaction after the Regency poppets who dominated male society in the early part of the century – by the 1840s Regency permissivity was out, and Victoria's family propriety religion was in). A witness to the

8. *ibid.*.

9. *Dante Alighieri*, Italian poet (1265-1321) wrote a Christian epic of the spirit in three cantos, *Inferno*, *Purgatorio* and *Paradiso*, in which man's eternal destiny is explained.

change in the idea of woman is found in Disraeli, who wrote on the great influence women can have on men's lives, – at the age of 76 he wrote a novel called *Endymion*, and said through the hero's words – "I owe everything to woman".

Little Dorrit is a part of the counter-theme, that is virtuous wholesome love against squalor, deception, criminality and evil. She has many qualities, such as the gift of being able to love, that is tenderness, or loving kindness – and to exercise this, one must have sympathy for people, and even more, empathy, the feeling for others' sufferings and problems. These qualities are revelatory and attractive, and it is no wonder Arthur Clennam falls in love with her. This is how Arthur sees her:

> Her purity and goodness came before him in their brightest light.[10]

Dickens mediates the idea with an image; he links the imaginative level of the intangible world of the spirit to a person – a poor young woman living in prison. But to correct the impression that Little Dorrit is the timid weak-willed conventional heroine of the run-of-the-mill novel of the time and note that she is a real person within the limits of fiction, we see she can defend herself, hold on to her own vision of what she is and wants, and induce respect for her own decisions. When her father would like her to marry John Chivers, the half-wit son of the jail's turnkey in return for favours he has received, she won't be given away as goods by her parent. Hers is a purity of purpose in life including self-respect. The image evoked of purity and goodness as a light is not new, but a forceful one in the foggy damp murk of poverty-stricken London. That she is not a vague symbolic creation is borne out by the fact that she is more than able to make direct purposive unconventional statements. When Arthur is ill in prison and she is away in Italy with her newly-rich family (Arthur helped her father to recover his inheritance and pay his debts and leave prison) she sends her "undying love" to him from her new life of comfort. Her love is strong, unashamed and open; she is emancipated enough to declare it, confirming that the earlier modesty was a chaste attitude and not one of class subjection i.e. the poor girl

10. Charles Dickens, *op. cit.* p.354.

abashed by the rich man. This first step of feminine emancipation is the first step in building up a relationship of mutual love with Arthur. Her heartfelt declaration of love seems to reveal Dickens' myth-destroying intentions (i.e. he is presenting an anti-conventional side to a young Victorian woman, distinguishing her from Fanny, her sister, who is portrayed as a social climber, who marries for position and money). Little Dorrit declares her true love for Arthur (who is a poor man, having lost his money in speculation by the end of the novel:

> I am rich in being taken by you.[11]

Arthur's love for her increases her love for him. The intersubjectivity makes the relationship valid, and her words above reflect a lyrical power to be found more frequently in the best English love lyrics. Love is thus shown as a spiritual richness. The proof that her love is true, and that she is modelled on an individual concept of personality is revealed in a letter to Arthur from Venice, in which she laments that her father has become rich, has servants, and that the family all live in luxury, but that there is also a formality grown up between them which did not exist when they were in prison, when her father spoke more intimately in a closer family atmosphere. Here, father, a representative Victorian, does not approve of a show of affection. She says:

> I have come to be at a distance from him; that even in the midst of all the servants and attendants, he is deserted and in want of me.[12]

The paradigmatic vocabulary portrays loss of communication, the sense of isolation, in the words – *distance*, *deserted*, *want*, all forms of separation, emptiness, need. Dickens thus shows that the spirit is a living dynamic force on which the individual depends for his psychic health. Little Dorrit's sincere love for Arthur is direct:

> It would break my heart to believe that you thought of me in any way that would make me stranger to you, than I was when you were so good to me.[13]

11. *ibid.* p.681.

12. *ibid.* p.392.

13. *ibid.* p.393.

Perhaps a more revelatory passage showing that Little Dorrit is not a cardboard character, a reductive or abstract symbol of purity and love is when Dickens allows his invention, his heroine to have a fault – (could we suspect irony here?) and that is when the Dorrits leave the Marshalsea. Her father pays all his debts but he is inevitably older by twenty years and to Little Dorrit it seems a harsh justice that makes him pay twice:

> It seems hard to me that he should pay in life and money both... ...Yes, I know I'm wrong, she pleaded timidly, don't think any worse of me; it has grown up with me here.[14]

Dickens' heroine is human, she has suffered, she has a sense of social justice, though she does not try to justify it – there is no resentment. But Dickens' authorial comment is telling, – suffering can destroy a human soul or at least warp it, – that is the indirect message:

> The prison which could spoil so many things, had tainted Little Dorrit's mind. No more than this.[15]

Little Dorrit is portrayed as a creature born to manifest love – a human love which is well-nigh perfect as to seem divinely inspired, but she is real flesh-and-blood and not blind to the world she lives in, not indifferent to social injustice and suffering. Her self-sacrifice, her abnegation born of prison and poverty does not conclude in bitterness. Again Dickens' authorial comment reveals that she is an ordinary young woman who, like any other girl of her age, needs clothes and shoes, and when Dorrit her father frets over his clothes, Dickens says:

> All this time [in prison that is] he never once thought of *her* dress, her shoes, her need of anything.[16]

Despite all, she loves her father, and would have 'laid down' her life for him.

Arthur Clennam has been referred to several times as the man whom Little Dorrit falls in love with, though he is much

14. *ibid.* p.353.

15. ditto

16. *ibid.* p. p.193.

older (he has spent twenty years in the East with his father, because he was an illegitimate son, and his adoptive mother, Mrs. Clennam uses him to punish his father, her husband, and Arthur by banishing them overseas). Arthur comes back to England after his father dies. He finds his life surrounded by mystery; the greatest of all being his believed mother's coldness and harshness towards life and himself in particular. Coming back after twenty years abroad, Arthur is alone in London without acquaintance, in a complicated and mysterious family situation. This makes him morally weak and powerless to act. His alienation from a mother who leads the life of a recluse in an old mouldering gloomy house in the miasmic atmosphere of the river Thames paralysed physically and mentally by strange superstitious religious fixations and repressions confuse him. Her character is a foil to Little Dorrit's. Mrs. Clennam's religion of an "eye for an eye" leads her to believe she has been appointed by God to vindicate the dishonourable position she has been led into by marrying a man who was already in love with a dancer who became Arthur's mother. Thus she takes on the responsibility of punishing Arthur's father and Arthur by banishing them to China, and making the dancer, Arthur's mother, relinquish all her rights over Arthur and his father, in exchange for respectability and maintenance both for herself and Arthur, who of course must be brought up as Mrs. Clennam's son, a

> predestined and lost boy, to give him the reputation of an honest origin; to bring him up in fear and trembling, and in a life of practical contrition for the sins that were heavy on his head before his entry into this condemned world. Was that cruelty? .... I was appointed to do these things.[17]

She explains herself to Little Dorrit in these terms when revealing part of the family mystery. Her terrible evil force manifests itself as a usurpation of the function of God in the name of a false religion and hypocritical morality. It destroys the lives of her own family, – and her evil is paralleled with the evil of social forces which conspire to ruin honest citizens who are gulled into making bad investments with their money. So, in a

17. *ibid.* p.649.

surprising long drawn-out dénouement, Arthur, a debtor, ends up in the Marshalsea prison, just, dramatically, not long after the Dorrits leave it, very rich, mainly through his efforts. Dickens introduces a sub-theme of financial scandal to provoke a crisis in the main theme: suspense is created by a reversal of fortune, the House of Clennam collapses literally when Little Dorrit has the mystery of Arthur revealed to her by Mrs. Clennam, who remains a dumb paralytic.

But Arthur is saved by love, and suffering. His purgatorial experience of poverty and prison and his realisation he is not alone and that people love him (he is helped by Mr. Meagles, a retired banker, and Mr. Doyce, an honest hard-working engineer and of course loved by Little Dorrit) lead him to renounce his alienating upbringing in a stern discipline, which was the strict Sabbatarian environment of Calvinistic inspiration of his childhood, and realise his inner self, a good person who suspects that his life must change for the better. However, his background is against him; he is the child of a kind of utilitarianism, and as he says, his parents were "professors of a stern religion", who had "austere faces, inexorable discipline, penance in this world and terror in the next". On his way back to England from the East, he meets Mr. Meagles, who becomes his friend (he and Doyce, another friend, an engineer representing the uncorrupt world of honest work, both pay Arthur's debts and get him out of the Marshalsea), and declares to him:

> So here I am, in the middle way, having had twenty years largely wasted...

Interestingly, these words remind the reader of the beginning of Dante's *Inferno* (Nel mezzo del cammin di nostra vita...) suggesting that Dickens wants to present a London, his London of the poor and the honest as a kind of Inferno of suffering, and more particularly the hell of the spiritual suffering of Arthur, confused and middle-aged as Dante was when he wrote the *Divine Comedy*. Here are Arthur's words:

> I have no will. That is to say... next to none that I can put into action now. Trained by main force... I was never consulted... shipped away to the other end of the world before I was of age, and exiled there until my father's death... always grinding in a mill I always hated;

what is to be expected from *me* in middle life? Will, purpose, hope? All these lights were extinguished before I could sound the words.[18]

Again the image of light, – used before by Dante and Coleridge[19] to represent the spirit, love, happiness. On one occasion, Arthur is listening to the Sunday church bells ringing all over London, deafening thought and action; he is alone in his room and remembers his boyhood unhappiness, – no childhood, no youth, except 'one remembrance' – a reference to the non-existence of love in his family. Arthur paradoxically comes out of this deprivation free from the usual Victorian social and religious prejudices:

Bred in meanness, and hard dealing, this had rescued him to be a man of honourable mind and open hand. Bred in coldness and severity, this had rescued him to have a warm and sympathetic heart. Bred in a creed too darkly audacious to pursue, through its process of reversing the making of man in the image of his Creator to the making of his Creator in the image of an erring man, this had rescued him to judge not, and in humility to be merciful, and have hope and charity.[20]

This authorial comment on Arthur gives us a clue to the real theme of the novel, – it is the presentation of the process of finding oneself, and the nature of spiritual freedom. It is a presentation of people through their actions and beliefs, how they act and choose in the course of their lives. The spirit is free to choose, to make the right or wrong moral choices. It is Dickens' view of London, the stage for a struggle between good and evil, seen in the lives of its citizens, some unhappy or poor or criminal and others definitely choosing to fight for some kind of spiritual serenity, against a distorted view of religion and man's social duty based in Victorian times on a rigid 'puritan' way of conduct. Other authors noted this too. J.S.Mill wrote about Calvinism in his *Essay on Liberty* (1859):

According to that [the Calvinistic theory] the one great offence of man is self-will. All the good of which humanity is capable is

18. *ibid.* p.17.

19 *Samuel Taylor Coleridge*, poet (1772-1834) wrote *The Ancient Mariner*, *Christabel* and *Kubla Kahn*.

20. Charles Dickens, *op. cit.* p.139.

> comprised in obedience. You have no choice; thus you must do, and not otherwise: "Whatever is not a duty is a sin". Human nature being radically corrupt, there is no redemption for anyone until human nature is killed within him.

Compare this with how Mrs. Clennam tyrannised over Arthur, "that the child might work out his release in bondage and hardship". She refuses to answer Arthur when he asks for information on the mystery he has been brought up in. His father's dying wish was that he bring back a watch with the initials D.N.F. on it – Do Not Forget. His adoptive mother was not to forget to explain something to him. Arthur gets no satisfaction, so he is troubled, he feels that restitution or reparation should be made to someone. This moral problem mystery with its undertones of guilt complex was the kind of enigma that fascinated the Victorian thinking public. Dickens is interested in presenting the psychological and spiritual effect of ideas, the determinism created by strong forces, such as religion in the case of Mrs. Clennam and Arthur. J.S.Mill is not the only writer to comment on determinism. Material environment too determines human character, a view presented by the reformer and philanthropist, Robert Owen[21]:

> Every day will make it more and more evident that the character of man is, without a single exception, always formed for him; that it may be, and is, chiefly, created by his predecessors; that they give him or may give him, his ideas and habits, which are the powers that govern and direct his conduct. Man, therefore, never did, nor is it possible he ever can, form his own character. (Third Essay, *A New View of Society*)

This is utilitarian determinism, not what Dickens was trying to do. Dickens was a radical humanist, bent on presenting the reasons behind choice and human action to show how free will is formed. However, Mrs. Clennam justifies herself in the terms of psychological and religious determinism. She answers Rigaud Blandois, a criminal who is blackmailing her through documents he possesses which reveal the secret of the House of

21. *Robert Owen* – Welsh industrialist and philanthropist (1771-1856), reduced the working day to ten and a half hours, instituted loans and pensions and co-operative selling for consumer goods through his policies.

Clennam, in this way:

> You do not know what it is... to be brought up strictly and straitly. I was so brought up. Mine was no light youth of sinful gaiety and pleasure. Mine were days of wholesome repression, punishment and fear[22].

Notice the use of the adjective "wholesome"; for Mrs. Clennam's perverted logic, her dire religion could only produce good effects – and paradoxically in Arthur's case it does. Dickens seems to affirm indirectly that we cannot blame outside forces for what happens in our minds – they are only partially responsible for what we are: Mrs. Clennam chooses a life of repression and unhappiness; Arthur chooses contact with people and spiritual freedom. Finally she is closed within herself, tormented and paralytic; and he, outgoing in action and willpower, is rewarded with happiness. He meets Little Dorrit, falls in love, and she too with him. Her love brings happiness for two souls searching for it. Their marriage confirms that love, married love, a Victorian and human ideal, can bring happiness – the conventional ending of many Victorian novels. Little Dorrit and Arthur get married in St. George's Church under a holy painting:

> And they were married, with the sun shining on them through the painted figure of Our Saviour on the window... Little Dorrit and her husband walked out of the church alone. They paused for a moment on the steps of the portico, looking at the fresh perspective of the street in the autumn morning sun's bright rays, and then went down....Went down into a modest life of usefulness and happiness.... They went quietly down into the roaring streets, inseparable and blessed: and as they passed along in sunshine and shade, the noisy and the eager, the arrogant and the froward and the vain, fretted and chafed and made their usual uproar.[23]

The world goes by, but two human souls have found each other and that is all we can expect of good fortune in life, Dickens affirms in these closing lines.

22. Charles Dickens, *op. cit* p.646.

23. *ibid.* p.687-8.